REINHOLD NIEBUHR

&

46

THE QUESTION OF

GLOBAL DEMOCRACY

Reinhold Niebuhr

&

the Question of Global Democracy

David Ray Griffin

PROCESS
CENTURY
PRESS

ANOKA, MINNESOTA 2021

Process Century Press
RiverHouse LLC
802 River Lane
Anoka, MN 55303

Process Century Press books are published in association with the International Process Network.

Cover: Susanna Mennicke

VOLUME VII
THEOLOGICAL EXPLORATIONS SERIES
JEANYNE B. SLETTOM, GENERAL EDITOR

ISBN 978-1-940447-49-0
Printed in the United States of America

This series aims to explore the implications of Whiteheadian philosophy and theology for religious belief and practice. It also proposes that process religious thinkers, working from within many different traditions—Buddhist, Confucian, Christian, Hindu, Indigenous, Jewish, Muslim, and others—have unique insights pertinent to the critical issues of our day.

In 1976, we published a book, *Process Theology: An Introductory Exposition,* in which we aimed to "show the creative potentiality of a process perspective in theology." In addition to its explanation of process concepts and their application to Christian doctrine, the book noted the contribution of Whiteheadian thought toward "intercultural and interreligious understanding" and took an early stance on the ecological threat, claiming that process theology was prepared to "make a distinctive contribution" to this challenge.

Since the publication of that book, we have seen many others explore these and other themes in articles, books, and conferences. At the same time, the threat to planetary health and the need for "intercultural and interreligious understanding" has only accelerated. This series is an effort to support theologians and religious philosophers in their ongoing exposition of possible Whiteheadian solutions.

John B. Cobb, Jr.
David Ray Griffin

OTHER BOOKS IN THIS SERIES

God of Empowering Love, David P. Polk
God Exists but Gawd Does Not, David Ray Griffin
Counter-Imperial Churching for a Planetary Gospel, Timothy Murphy
Process Theology, David Ray Griffin
The Christian Gospel for Americans, David Ray Griffin
Salvation, John B. Cobb, Jr.

Table of Contents

Acknowledgments,i
Preface, iii

One: Anarchical Civilization and Its Discontents, 1

Two: Early Plans to End War: From Dante to the
         Concert of Europe, 9

Three: The League of Nations and Its Failure, 21

Four: The United Nations and Its Failure, 29

Five: Reinhold Niebuhr on Global Government, 41

Six: Against the Three-fold Veto of Global Democracy, 111

Endnotes, 151
Index, 189

Acknowledgments

Chapter 5, "Reinhold Niebuhr on Global Government," this book's central chapter, was written some years ago while I was on sabbatical leave in Oxford. I am indebted to Keith Ward, who with his wife Marian served as my host at Christ Church, one of Oxford's major colleges.

Chapter 4, "The United Nations and Its Failure," was previously published simply as "The United Nations" in my book *The American Trajectory: Divine or Demonic?* (Clarity Press, 2018).

I am grateful to Jeanyne Slettom, the editor of Process Century Press, for whipping my manuscript into shape for publication. She had published some of my previous books. But I am particularly grateful for her work on this book, because the manuscript was especially challenging.

As always, I am mainly indebted to my wife, Ann Jaqua, for her indispensible help. For example, she made it possible for me to spend much of my time in Oxford studying and writing about Niebuhr's books.

Preface

In 1973, I wrote an essay in which I examined Reinhold Niebuhr's philosophical-theological-ethical position from a Whiteheadian perspective.[1] I gave a very positive appraisal, suggesting, in effect, that Whiteheadians could adopt Niebuhr's ethical position as their own, thereby enriching their writings about social ethics. I later became more critical.

Central to my criticism involved his attitude to global democracy. Whereas his interest declined, mine grew. Therefore, it has been gratifying to see, in this century, that there has been a growing interest in global democracy, as evidenced by the following books: Didier Jacobs, *Global Democracy: The Struggle for Political and Civil Rights in the 21st Century* (Vanderbilt University Press, 2007); Torbjörn Tännsjö, *Global Democracy: The Case for a World Government* (Edinburgh University Press, 2008); Daniele Archibugi, *The Global Commonwealth of Citizens: Toward Cosmopolitan Democracy* (Princeton University Press, 2008); Walter F. Baber and Robert V. Bartlett, *Global Democracy and Sustainable Jurisprudence: Deliberative Environmental Law* (MIT Press 2009); *Global Democracy: Normative and Empirical Perspectives,* ed. by Daniele Archibugi, Mathias Koenig-Archibugi, and Raffaele Marchetti (Cambridge University Press, 2012); Jo Leinen & Andreas Bummel, *A World Parliament: Governance and Democracy in the 21st Century* (Democracy Without Borders, 2018); Glen T. Martin, *Global Democracy and Human Self-Transcendence: The Power of the Future for Planetary Transformation* (Cambridge Scholars Publishing, 2018); Catherine Eschle, *Global Democracy, Social Movements, and Feminism* (Routledge, 2019).

At the same time, this century has seen unprecedented assaults on the idea of democracy itself. These events are serious enough on their own, but they are occuring within the context of a global climate emergency. It is in light of these events that I add this book to the growing calls for global democracy.

1

Anarchical Civilization and Its Discontents

In *Civilization and Its Discontents*, Freud argued famously that civilization as such is in strong tension with human nature, especially its libidinal dimension, so that civilized existence is inevitably a deeply discontented existence. Be that as it may, the argument of the present book is that the chief problem facing human beings today is not civilization as such but its *anarchical* character.

The discontents to which anarchical civilization has given rise involve frustrations not to our libidos but to our desires for a just, democratic, peaceable mode of existence, even our desire that human civilization itself will not perish in the foreseeable future.

More particularly, the discontents produced by anarchical civilization, which are becoming increasingly intolerable to increasing numbers of people, include our discontent with a world in which the richest one percent of the human race is becoming increasingly wealthy while the majority is becoming increasingly impoverished, with millions of people, including children, dying every year for lack of food or water. We are also discontent with a world in which over a trillion dollars is spent annually for military security while the deteriorating ecological security of the planet—especially the climate change produced by global warming, the warming and acidification of the oceans, and the increasingly rapid loss of species—are ignored on the grounds that the cures would be too expensive.

The diagnosis offered here—that the anarchical character of civilization is at the root of these discontents—is not yet common-place. Part of the reason is that we tend not to notice causal factors that have always been there, and civilization, from its origin some 12,000 years ago until the present, has always been anarchical. Another reason is that diagnoses of our current ailments usually lift up those causes that can be overcome, and the fact that civilization has always been anarchical has led most commentators to assume that it always will be.

The argument of the present book, by contrast, is that this anarchy *can* be overcome and that, if human civilization is to have a bright future, perhaps any future at all, it *must* be overcome.

Anarchy and Sovereignty

In popular language, the term "anarchy" is often used to refer to a chaotic situation, such as a riot, in which there is a complete breakdown of law and order. In the present book, however, the term is used in its literal sense to mean a realm in which there is no political authority. (The term is based on the Greek *anarkhia*, which comes from *anarkhos*, meaning "without a ruler.") The realm in question here is the international realm, which involves the relations among the various nation-states.[1]

To speak of the "international anarchy"[2] is simply to say that there is no global government over and above the governments of the various countries that could regulate their relations with each other. To grasp the full meaning of this international anarchy, it is necessary to grasp its reverse side, which is the idea that each country is a sovereign state.

The idea of state sovereignty is the idea of the state as the *supreme law-giving and law-enforcing authority* within a particular territory. Sovereignty thus understood is a primarily legal-political idea involving a claim about the *status* of the state—the claim that it has ultimate legislative, judicial, and executive authority over the people and resources of the territory in question. As such, sovereignty differs from *autonomy*, which involves the actual power or freedom of the state to control its own internal life without interference from outside. Although some theorists have characterized this distinction as that between two types of sovereignty—such as *formal* and *operational* sovereignty—it is less confusing if the term "sovereignty" is used solely to refer to the legal-political status, with some other term—such as *autonomy, freedom*, or *power*—used for the actual capacity to exercise the claim to sovereignty.[3]

To understand and evaluate this idea of sovereignty, it is helpful to know its background. The word itself comes from the French term *souverain*, which meant "a supreme ruler not accountable to anyone, except perhaps to God."[4] The concept behind the word had theological roots in the traditional idea of divine sovereignty, according to which God, by virtue of having absolute power, had the right to absolute dominion over the world.[5] When combined with other theological ideas, such as human beings as embodying the *imago Dei* and some human beings as specially designated *representatives* of God, this concept of divine sovereignty led to the idea of earthly rulers with analogous powers.

For example, Jean Bodin, who in the sixteenth century developed the first full-blown theory of sovereignty,[6] said that "it is the distinguishing mark of the sovereign that he cannot in any way be subject to the commands of another, for it is he who makes law for the subjects."[7] This idea of sovereignty came to be attributed to the state.

The notion of state sovereignty has two dimensions, internal and external. The idea of *internal* sovereignty means that the state, in distinction from any other associations *within* the territory in question, has a *monopoly on the legitimate exercise of coercive power.* When sovereignty in this sense was attributed to the state by Bodin in the sixteenth century and by Thomas Hobbes in the seventeenth, the "state" was essentially equated with the monarch. This idea of state sovereignty was "developed as an instrument for the assertion of royal authority over feudal princes."[8]

This assertion was, Tomaz Mastnak pointed out, "a response to the social violence ravaging late medieval and early modern Europe."[9] The effective assertion of sovereignty in this sense required the territory's "pacification," in the sense of disarming all other associations, at least sufficiently to prevent them from presenting a threat to the state's power to keep the peace within its borders. The conception of sovereignty as formulated by Bodin and Hobbes was oriented around this internal meaning.

In discussions of international relations, however, the focus is on the notion of *external* sovereignty, which means that "independence of outside authority in the control of territory and population [is] the inherent right of all states."[10] Although the idea of sovereignty developed by Bodin and Hobbes was not explicitly applied to the relations *among* nations until the eighteenth century,[11] the roots of this external application are usually seen to lie in the Peace of Westphalia of 1648, which affirmed the principle *cujus regio ejus religio,* according to which each monarch had the right to determine the religion of his or her own region. Bringing to a close the Thirty Years War, which actually culminated about 150 years of religious warfare, the Westphalian accords were intended to make each state free from religiously motivated interventions by other states and the papacy.

When theorists in the eighteenth and nineteenth centuries developed the notion of external sovereignty, they were generalizing the Westphalian principle, which stipulates that the state is not subject to any *religious* authority, to say that the state is not subject to *any* authority beyond itself whatsoever, so that no external power has the right to stipulate how it is to treat its citizens.[12] The Peace of Westphalia, say Thomas Weiss and Jarat Chopra,[13] "transferred to nation-states the special godlike features of church authority. States inherited sovereignty, and with it an unassailable position above the law that has since remained the central element of international relations." The system based upon this idea of sovereignty is commonly referred to as the Westphalian world order.

It is this order, with its lack of a global government over and above the governments of the various countries, to which this book applies the term "anarchy."

Anarchy and Political Realism

In the political field known as International Relations, this usage is commonplace. For example, in an essay in a volume entitled *The Perils of Anarchy*, Christopher Layne wrote:

> International politics is an anarchic, self-help realm.
> 'Anarchy,' rather than denoting chaos or rampant disorder,
> refers in international politics to the fact that there is no
> central authority capable of making and enforcing rules
> of behavior on the international system's units (states).[14]

Although this usage is widespread among theorists of international politics, the fact and the implications of international anarchy are especially emphasized by the school of thought known as (Political) Realism,[15] which insists that international relations are based on power, self-interest, competition, and self-help (*not* on moral norms, the general good, cooperation, and common security). For example, in the preface to *The Perils of Anarchy*, which is oriented around the Realist approach to international politics, we read:

> Realists regard anarchy—the absence of any common sovereign—as the distinguishing feature of international life. Without a central authority to enforce agreements or to guarantee security, states must rely on their own means to protect their interests.[16]

One of the contributors to that volume, John Mearsheimer, wrote:

> The international system is anarchic. This does not mean that it is chaotic or riven by disorder. It is easy to draw that conclusion, since Realism depicts a world characterized by security competition and war. However, "anarchy" as employed by Realists has nothing to do with conflict; rather, it is an ordering principle, which says that the system comprises independent political units (states) that have no central authority over them. Sovereignty, in other words, inheres in states, because there is no higher ruling body in the international system. There is no "government over governments."[17]

Likewise, in describing "the 'Realist' theory of international politics," David Held wrote:

> Realism posits that the system of sovereign states is inescapably anarchic in character; and that this anarchy forces all states, in the inevitable absence of any supreme arbiter to enforce moral behaviour and agreed international codes, to pursue power politics in order to attain their vital interests.[18]

Political Realists, besides emphasizing the fact and implications of international anarchy, also typically believe it to be a permanent feature of human civilization, at least a feature destined to persist for another century or so. This latter point, it should be emphasized, is distinct from, and not necessarily implied by, the former points. That is, one might well agree with the Realist account of the centrality of anarchy in international politics and the implications thereof, but not agree with the claim that we must continue, at least for the time being, to put up with what Realists themselves recognize to be "the perils of anarchy." There have been, in fact, a few Realists who have advocated the creation of a global government. For most Realists, however, recognition of the need to resign ourselves to this fate is part and parcel of the very meaning of Realism. The idea that we could transcend international anarchy by creating a "government above governments," at least in the near future, is considered *utopian* in the most pejorative sense of the term. For most Realists, to be realistic is to hold that the creation of a global government would be impossible (at least soon enough for present efforts in this direction to be worthwhile—a qualification that should henceforth always be taken as implied).

2

Early Plans to End War

From Dante to the Concert of Europe

T HE CENTRAL QUESTION created by the international realm, with its anarchical order, is whether it can be tamed so as to prevent perpetual warfare, or whether this result can be attained only by modifying the international realm so as to overcome its anarchy. The latter would mean having a higher authority that would put limits on each state's external sovereignty. This chapter looks primarily at thinkers in earlier centuries who believed that the perpetual threat of war could be overcome only by such a modification.

Dante Alighieri

The idea that the world needed a structure with which to prevent war was enunciated already in the Middle Ages.[1] The most famous of the early proposals, made in the fourteenth century, was *De Monarchia,* by Dante Alighieri. Arguing that princes cannot be judged by other princes of the same rank, because they are competitors, Dante advocated a world-state under an all-powerful emperor. Because there would be nothing to tempt the appetite of such an emperor, Dante said, "in him there may be judgment and justice more strongly than in any other."[2] This emperor would impartially enforce a universal law.[3]

Although we, with our awareness of Lord Acton's dictum—"Power tends to corrupt, and absolute power corrupts absolutely"[4]—may be skeptical of Dante's solution to the problem of anarchy, he certainly recognized one of the conditions for fair arbitration of disputes between two rulers. The decision must be made by a *disinterested* party rather than by one of the parties to the dispute or even a third party that could benefit from the decision.

Émeric Crucé

In 1623, a monk named Émeric Crucé published a discourse on the "means to establish a general peace." Arguing that we needed a way of life befitting human beings, he appealed to the monarchs to create a world government, through which the world could be ruled by reason and justice, "and not violence, which is only suited to the beasts." Disputes between rulers would be settled by an assembly of ambassadors representing all the rulers.[5]

Thomas Hobbes

Much more influential, however, were two writers of the seventeenth century who made no effort to put an end to war. One of these was Thomas Hobbes, whose most famous work was entitled *Leviathan* (1651). Describing an anarchical realm in which there is no supreme ruler as a "state of nature," Hobbes used the international realm as his major illustration of a state of nature. Although he regarded this realm as a completely lawless realm of perpetual war—in the sense that any state *could* be attacked by any other state at any time—he made no proposal for overcoming this lawlessness. It had been necessary, he believed, for *individuals* to escape the state of nature by submitting themselves to a sovereign ruler (a "leviathan") within a territorial state. He argued, however, that the dangers created by the lawlessness of the international realm were not sufficiently intolerable to necessitate the creation of a *universal* sovereign to which the states would submit.[6]

Hugo Grotius

Another highly influential writer of the seventeenth century was Hugo Grotius, who published *The Rights of War and Peace* in 1625. In describing his motivation, Grotius said:

> I observed everywhere in Christendom a lawlessness in warfare of which even barbarous nations would be ashamed. Nations would rush to arms on the slightest pretext or even without cause at all. And arms once taken up, there would be an end to all respect for law, whether human or divine, as though a fury had been let loose with general license for all manner of crime.[7]

Grotius did not, however, try to prevent war. He tried only to humanize it. But his principles arguably did not even do that.

Jean-Jacques Rousseau, later complaining that Grotius was widely "praised to the skies" while "Hobbes [was] covered with execration," said that in reality "their principles are exactly alike." Grotius, he said, could not have produced a philosophy "more favorable to tyrants."[8] One reason for this judgment was that Grotius, believing that most rulers could be trusted to enforce both the law of nations and the law of nature (the moral law) fairly, called on rulers to punish those who violated them.[9]

John Locke

Writing at the end of the seventeenth century, John Locke, like Dante before him, said that individuals in conflictual situations could *not* be trusted to apply the moral law impartially, because they would all interpret the law to their own advantage. Although Locke did not explicitly apply this principle to the international realm, he did refer to the relation between sovereigns as a state of nature.[10] Locke's insight therefore implied, as Cornelius Murphy said in his *Theories of World Governance*, the impossibility of "the unprejudiced enforcement of the fundamental law, which was an indispensable part of the whole Grotian system."[11]

William Penn

Probably the first truly practicable plan for overcoming war was *An Essay towards the Present and Future Peace of Europe*, published by William Penn in 1693. Arguing, like several before him, that Christendom's reputation could be recovered only if it learns to settle its disputes peaceably, Penn proposed that the European princes form a parliament that would formulate rules of justice, then meet regularly to settle disputes. Voting would be by secret ballot (to avoid bribery—a principle the League of Nations and the United Nations later should have embodied). Although Penn was a Quaker, he said that force would need to be used against any princes who refused to join, or to submit differences to the Parliament, or to abide by its rulings.

Although the Parliament would not destroy any country's (internal) sovereignty, Penn said, it would make it so that "the great Fish can no longer eat up the little ones." This plan, he pointed out, would also prevent the needless destruction of lives, cities, and countries. It would also, thanks to the disarmament it would allow, save enormous amounts of money.[12]

Jean-Jacques Rousseau

In 1713, Abbé de Saint-Pierre had published *A Project for Settling an Everlasting Peace in Europe*. In 1761, Jean-Jacques Rousseau published a so-called *Abstract* of this work, followed (posthumously) by *Judgment on Saint-Pierre's Project for Perpetual Peace* in 1782. From this and his other writings, especially *The State of War*, Rousseau's position can be summarized in the following points:[13]

1. The misery created by war is so great that a plan to secure lasting peace must be found.

2. Recurrent war is evitable as long as states have absolute (external) sovereignty.

3. Perpetual peace will be possible only on the basis of a federation with (a) laws to promote the common good, (b) a court and a parliament in which disputes can be settled, and (c) armed strength sufficient to enforce these rulings.

4. The advantages of this system will so outweigh its disadvantages, even from the perspective of the princes—they would, for example, be able to put an end to the ever-increasing cost of military preparations—that if they could distinguish their real from their apparent interest, they would adopt it.[14]

Rousseau knew, however, that princes might be unable to make this distinction and hence would reject his proposed federation because it would take away their "precious right to be unjust as they please." It would also take away "the apparatus of power and terror with which they love to frighten the world" and with which they can reap honors from "the glory of conquest."[15]

Immanuel Kant

If Rousseau was the first major philosopher to advocate a plan for overcoming war, Immanuel Kant—who greatly admired Rousseau—was the second. Although most Kant scholars have not focused on this dimension of his thought, it was actually the major concern of Kant's writings in his final years.[16] Most important for our purposes is the tension between Kant's best-known statements on this subject, contained in *Perpetual Peace* and *The Metaphysics of Morals*, which were published in 1796 and 1797, respectively,[17] and the position he had articulated a few years earlier.

In *Perpetual Peace*, he advocated the creation of a "pacific federation," which would extend gradually to encompass all states. "This federation [would not have] any power like that of a state," so the confederated states would *not* "need to submit to public laws and to a coercive power which enforces them."[18] In *The Metaphysics of Morals*, Kant made the point even clearer, saying that "this association must not embody a sovereign power as in a civil constitution, but only a partnership or *confederation*. It must therefore be an alliance that can be terminated at any time."[19]

In earlier writings, however, Kant had said the opposite. In 1784, three years after the appearance of *The Critique of Pure Reason*, he published *The Idea for a Universal History with a Cosmopolitan Purpose*, in which he said that people, through war, will be driven to abandon a lawless state of savagery and enter

> a federation of peoples in which every state . . . could expect to derive its security and rights not from its own power . . . but solely from . . . a united power and the law-governed decisions of a united will. However wild and fanciful this idea may appear—and it has been ridiculed as such when put forward by the Abbé St. Pierre and Rousseau . . . it is nonetheless the inevitable outcome of the distress in which men involve one another. For this distress must force the states to make exactly the same decisions . . . as that which man was forced to make, equally unwillingly, in his savage state—the decision to renounce his brutish freedom and seek calm and security within a law-governed constitution.[20]

As this statement shows, Kant at that time was saying that warfare could be overcome through a federation with a constitution, a "united power," and a "united will." The step thought unnecessary by Hobbes—in which states, analogously to individuals, would leave the lawless state of nature by subordinating themselves to a higher authority, thereby giving up some freedom to gain security—was by Kant said to be necessary.

In a later essay, Kant, after saying that "a permanent universal peace by means of a so-called *European balance of power* is a pure illusion," argued that the distress produced by wars must finally lead the states, "even against their will, to enter into a *cosmopolitan* constitution."[21] But Kant cautioned against a universal monarch, adding:

> Or if such a state of universal peace is in turn even more dangerous to freedom, for it may lead to the most fearful despotism…distress must force men to form a state which is not a cosmopolitan commonwealth under a single ruler, but a lawful *federation* under a commonly accepted *international right.*[22]

Whatever exactly Kant meant by this, he still intended that such a federation would be "based upon enforceable public laws to which each state must submit (by analogy with a state of civil or political right among individual men)."[23] Kant thereby still endorsed what has come to be called the "domestic analogy," a world government that is analogous to a domestic (national) government.[24]

With this background, we can now look more closely at Kant's still later statement in *Perpetual Peace*, according to which the federation would *not* have power to coerce the individual states. Although this vision has generally been taken as Kant's preferred position, he actually offered it as merely a "negative substitute" for his positive vision of a world republic, which would be the best option. In discussing this best option, he said:

There is only one rational way in which states coexisting with other states can emerge from the lawless condition of pure warfare. Just like individual men, they must renounce their savage and lawless freedom, adapt themselves to public coercive laws, and thus form an *international state*.[25]

Kant clearly said that this approach, which involves the domestic analogy, is the *only* rational way to escape from the lawless state of nature. But Kant then made a fateful concession, saying:

But since this is not the will of the nations... the positive idea of a *world republic* cannot be realised. If all is not to be lost, this can at best find a negative substitute in the shape of an enduring and gradually expanding *federation* likely to prevent war. The latter may check the current of man's inclination to defy the law and antagonise his fellows, although there will always be a risk of it bursting forth anew.[26]

As this statement shows, Kant suggested his "negative substitute" only because a "world republic," which is what was really needed, was not "the will of the nations." By "nations" he did not mean the people—this was before the age of democracy—but the "great statesmen" and the "heads of state," who, he had complained in his 1792 essay, always ridicule proposals of the type put forth by Abbé Saint-Pierre and Rousseau.[27]

Kant knew, moreover, that this substitute, being devoid of coercive power, could not guarantee an end to war but was at best "likely" to prevent it. He probably even knew that the word "likely" was an exaggeration. He knew, in any case, that with such a federation "there will always be a risk of [war] bursting forth anew."

Kant thereby settled for a compromise that could not guarantee perpetual peace. He would have many followers.

William Ladd

Although European politicians showed no inclination to adopt the schemes of Penn, Rousseau, or Kant (even his water-downed version), thinkers who saw the need to overcome war kept making proposals. One of these was William Ladd, who in 1828 had founded the American Peace Society. In 1840, he published *An Essay on a Congress of Nations for the Adjustment of International Disputes without Resort to Arms*, which became very influential in both America and England.

Rejecting the Hobbesian dictum that "covenants without swords are but words," Ladd believed that previous leagues for peace had failed because they did rely on the power of the sword. Accordingly, although his proposal called for congressional and judicial bodies, he said that the executive was to be public opinion, "the queen of the world." Once public opinion was enlightened, he suggested, its moral pressure would lead politicians to settle their disputes with reason instead of violence.[28]

James Lorimer

A more realistic proposal was put forward near the end of the century by James Lorimer, a Scottish legal philosopher, in *The Institutes of the Law of Nations*.[29] He was convinced that the relatively peaceful international relations that had characterized the nineteenth century would not continue without disarmament. He also argued that disarmament would not occur without the prior creation of an international government with the necessary military forces to provide security. The society of states would, however, not be undermined.[30] The international government would, in fact, be "the guardian of the freedom of all national governments."[31]

This international government would have its own legislature (consisting of a senate and a chamber of deputies), its own judiciary (with civil and criminal branches), and its own executive. It would also, in order to have the capacity to protect the freedom of the states, have its own power to tax and its own standing army.[32] Lorimer's proposal, accordingly, incorporated the domestic analogy in a strong sense.

However, said Cornelius Murphy, the proposals made by Lorimer and like-minded thinkers were not taken seriously: "the prevailing opinion in the late nineteenth century was that an international order could be achieved without the establishment of any permanent authority above the autonomous states."[33]

Nicolas Murray Butler and Lassa Oppenheim

An example of this optimism in the English-speaking world was provided by Nicolas Murray Butler's book *The International Mind*, in which he wrote:

> The civilized world is at peace and there is no ruler and no party bent on disturbing that peace. The more powerful nations are presided over by governments or monarchs whose faces are turned toward the light. . . . The German Emperor, against whom criticisms are sometimes leveled, is, I dare assert with confidence, a convinced believer in the policies of peace.[34]

This was published in 1913, one year before World War I broke out.

For an example of this optimism in the German-speaking world, we can turn to Lassa Oppenheim, a respected international lawyer who in 1911 published a book later translated as *The Future of International Law*.[35] According to Oppenheim, world government was unnecessary because the world was already a *society* of states, in which the independence of the members could be reconciled with the common interest of the whole human community. The law of nations would flourish when the principle of equality was more fully recognized, allowing the principle of "one state, one vote" to become operative. This was already happening, Oppenheim thought, so the traditional predominance of a minority of powerful states would soon be superseded.[36]

This happy development would occur, Oppenheim argued, because states are more moral than individuals and because unlimited progress is a law of the universe. Accordingly, the international interests of states would soon become stronger than their national interests.

However, Murphy pointed out, while Oppenheim was drawing inspiration from the Hague Peace conferences, he was ignoring the political theory of the state that had been vigorously defended at those meetings.

> Diplomats emphasized the supremacy of the nation rather than the general interests in peace and disarmament. . . . Lip service was given to pacific ideas. But while states, through their representatives, were posing as moral entities, they were reinforcing their separate military power and increasing their capacity for unilateral action. . . . At the time of Oppenheim's optimistic prognosis neither disarmament, nor the pacific adjustment of differences, were of paramount importance to the leading European powers.[37]

The Concert of Europe

Just as these "leading European powers" ignored Lorimer's proposal at the end of the nineteenth century, they had ignored the proposals of Rousseau and Kant at the end of the prior century. Since 1815, after the defeat of Napoleon at Waterloo, issues related to war and peace had been largely determined by an informal alliance of Great Powers (at first Great Britain, Russia, Prussia, and Austria, with France and Italy added later).

At some point this alliance—which in reality "enjoyed no more than intermittent existence"—became known as the Concert of

Europe.[38] It attempted to maintain peace by means of a balance of power[39]—an approach that Kant had warned would never bring lasting peace. The Concert had to rely entirely on power because it had "no provision for curbing the primacy of the national interest."[40]

The nineteenth century was, in comparison with previous centuries, relatively peaceful. There were, nevertheless, significant wars. One of these, the Franco-Prussian war of 1870–71, resulted in the emergence of the German Empire (which then took Prussia's place in the Concert). From then on, the Concert's basic problem—how to reconcile the competition between national interests with the desire for the avoidance of armed conflict—became increasingly difficult.[41] Meetings became less frequent.[42] The last meeting of the Concert was in 1913, meaning there was no meeting in 1914, the year World War I broke out.[43]

3

The League of Nations
and Its Failure

IN HIS HISTORY of the League of Nations, F. S. Northedge said: "The war which broke out in Europe in August 1914 was a bolt from the blue."[1] British political theoretician David Mitrany wrote that later generations "can hardly realize what a shock [the First World War] was," coming as it did after "a long period of stability and of liberal optimism."[2] This shock produced new thinking in many minds.

In 1923, British law professor George Keeton, in a book entitled *National Sovereignty and International Order*, wrote:

> Whereas only a few years before many publicists thought that the Hague Peace Conferences had ushered in a new era in international relationships . . . and while they were unanimous that the respect for international law was firmly based upon a public opinion whose censure would be sufficient to deter the potential lawbreaker, the war had made it necessary to abandon these doctrines.[3]

Even a chastened Lassa Oppenheim wrote in 1920, in his book's third edition, that the world needed an "international Parliament with power to legislate by a majority," a Permanent Court of International Justice with mandatory jurisdiction, and "an international Army and Navy to serve as a police force."[4]

Some prominent Americans agreed. In 1916, President Woodrow Wilson, speaking at the first convention of the League to Enforce Peace, declared:

> The world is even now upon the eve of a great consummation, when . . . coercion shall be summoned not to the service of political ambition or selfish hostility, but to the service of a common order, a common justice, and a common peace.[5]

He later said: "There must be, not a balance of power, but a community of power, not organized rivalries, but an organized common peace."[6]

Now that we have reached the limit of voluntary arbitration of disputes, said Senator Henry Cabot Lodge, "the next step is . . . to put force behind international peace."[7]

Former president Theodore Roosevelt devoted much of his 1915 book, *America and the World War*, to a proposal for a league for peace, saying: "If it is a Utopia, it is a Utopia of a very practical kind."[8]

The Launching of the League

New thinking of this type prepared the way for the creation of the League of Nations in 1920, as stipulated by the Treaty of Versailles in 1919. The League, as Northedge put it,

> was launched on the tide of revulsion, not only against the war just ended, but against all war, which swept the world when the fighting stopped in November 1918.[9]

The question was whether this revulsion would be sufficient to persuade the Great Powers to give up what Rousseau had mockingly called their "precious right to be unjust when they please."[10] This question was largely answered in advance by developments in the two strongest countries, Great Britain and the United States, who together were most responsible for the failure of the League.

How Great Britain Contributed to the League's Failure

The greatest influence on official British thinking was *International Government*, a book written in 1915 by Leonard Woolf (Virginia's husband) as the proposal of the Fabian Society. In the Introduction, George Bernard Shaw, another Fabian, said that putting an end to international anarchy, with its war, would depend upon a "supernational sheriff" to "adjust the disputes of nations." What is needed, Shaw argued, is "a Supernational Legislature, a Supernational Tribunal, and a Supernational Board of Conciliation."[11]

In the book itself, however, Woolf made clear from the outset that he was not proposing any fundamental change of the international structure: "If we are to [conceive of] a definite international organization which will commend itself to the disillusioned judgment of statesmen and other 'practical' men," Woolf declared, "we must build not a Utopia upon the air or clouds of our own imaginations, but a duller and heavier structure placed logically upon the foundations of the existing system." We cannot change this system, he argued, because of "the theoretical sacredness of the independence and the sovereignty of independent and sovereign States." His scheme, he said, "falls far short of a cosmopolitan system or a world state," because "every state must remain absolute master of its own destiny."[12]

Arguing that the world was not forced to choose between Utopia and Chaos, Woolf presented his proposed International Authority as a "half-way house between a federation into a world-State and the existing splendid isolation of independent States."[13] For this International Authority to work, he pointed out, the nations composing it must "agree to enforce, and actually enforce, by every means in their power the obligation of each independent State to refer a dispute or difference to the [Authority] before resorting to force of arms."[14]

To the criticism that this system would provide no guarantee against war, Woolf replied that "it is impossible to make war impossible" so we must settle for a plan that would "go far towards . . . making war extremely improbable." However, he admitted, each State would remain "quite free to go to war, in the last resort."[15]

This admission made most unrealistic Woolf's statement about disarmament, namely, that "national disarmament . . . is left to come about of itself, just as the individual carrying of arms falls silently into desuetude as and when fears of aggression die down before the rule of the law."[16] This was so unrealistic because the "international government" being proposed by Woolf was not at all analogous to a national government such as England's, which did make its citizens feel safe.

In any event, the main features of Woolf's proposal, which virtually admitted defeat in advance—being in essence the same as Kant's "negative substitute"—became incorporated into a memorandum drafted by the British Foreign Office, which then became the basis for the British position in the final Anglo-American negotiations prior to Versailles.[17] The British Empire, after losing almost a million of its citizens in World War I, would not even *propose* the creation of an organization with the power to prevent future wars from breaking out.

How the US Contributed to the League's Failure

The United States contributed to the failure of the League of

Nations in two ways. First, whereas the French, holding that "covenants without swords" are futile, wanted the League to have an international military force at its disposal, the Americans, like the British, would not endorse this idea. President Wilson argued that peace-loving world public opinion, backed up with the threat of economic sanctions, would be sufficient to prevent war.[18] Accordingly, when the League's Council was created, it was "an essentially deliberative body" rather than a peace-keeping or peace-restoring body. The decisions of the League "were recommendations only and carried no binding force." Accordingly, the later condemnation of the League as "the Geneva talking shop" was made virtually inevitable by its charter.[19]

Also, in order to avoid a veto by the US Senate, Wilson insisted—even while recognizing the absurdity of the demand—that the Covenant stipulate that it would not affect "the validity of . . . regional understandings like the Monroe Doctrine."[20] This stipulation entailed that the United States could do as it pleased in Latin America with no censure from the League.[21]

America's other major contribution to the failure of the League was the fact that, although Wilson had gotten the various demands of the US Senate built into the League's Covenant, the Senate then refused to ratify it.[22]

The US Senate's refusal to ratify was based in part on politics. Republican Henry Cabot Lodge, the head of the Senate Foreign Relations Committee, wanted to undermine the pet project of the Democrat Wilson. But the Senate's refusal to ratify the Covenant was also based on the desire of many of its more imperialistic members, such as Albert Beveridge and Lodge himself, not to allow any restrictions whatsoever on US freedom of action. The strength of that sentiment is shown by the fact that Democratic Senator John Sharp Williams spoke against it, denouncing those Senators who say: "I want my nation left free and untrammeled to do whatever it please."[23] Williams then asked rhetorically:

What would become of a municipal society composed of individuals founded upon that sort of basis? Suppose the Senator from Utah . . . went out and said: "I decline to be trammeled; I decline to enter into an agreement to abide by the pistol-toting law, or by the homicide law, or by the thievery law. . . . I will do right myself. I am my own sovereign, responsible to nobody but God." . . . Could you get civilization in a State out of citizens of that persuasion? Suppose each State in the Union said that to the other States of the Union? Could you get civilization in the American Union out of that? Why is it that thus far you have never gotten any civilization in the international world? Just simply because one nation after another, in blind chauvinism, has uttered that infernal, stupid selfishness.[24]

Although Williams' argument was unanswerable, the motion to ratify the League was defeated.[25] As a result, the League of Nations had to try to maintain world peace without the nation that had become the world's greatest economic and military power.

The Resulting Failure of the League

Not having the United States as a member surely contributed to the League's inability to achieve its major goals of keeping the peace and bringing about a general disarmament, as many commentators have said. But even if America had been in the League, the results would probably have not been greatly different, due to weaknesses built into the Covenant.

One of these weaknesses was Article 5, which stipulated that "decisions at any meeting of the Assembly or of the Council shall require the agreement of all the Members of the League represented at the meeting." This article meant that every state—not just the Great Powers—had a veto. As a result, resolutions were generally watered down until they were innocuous.

Equally important, because the League had no supranational

legislature, executive, or army, "The League was not going to impose order from above—there was no-one in the world to do that; order would have to come from below."[26]

In particular, it was up to the individual members of the League to decide if another member was violating the Covenant. If the answer was Yes, it was then up to the individual nations to provide the money and armed forces to stop the action. So although there were more rules than there were during the period of the Concert of Europe, "it rested with states whether they would make much or little of the new arrangements."[27] And they made little of them.

One consequence of the League's weakness was that "multilateral disarmament, which it was fervently believed the League would bring about," did not even begin, because disarmament would presuppose "foolproof collective security."[28] This obvious truth, emphasized by James Lorimer decades earlier, was finally recognized in a resolution, passed in 1922, declaring:

> [I]n the present state of the world, many Governments would be unable to accept the responsibility for a serious reduction of armaments unless they received in exchange a satisfactory guarantee of the safety of their country.[29]

This the League could not supply, so although there was no issue on which the League spent more time and energy than disarmament, its efforts came to nought.[30]

The ultimate failure of these efforts occurred in a world conference on disarmament that, after much dawdling, finally began in 1932. The world's interest in the conference was intense:

> The tables were loaded with millions of petitions from people yearning for peace all over the world. The churches rang with prayers for the long-awaited talks.[31]

But this conference, in which each country focused on maximizing its own advantages, disbanded in failure in 1934. This failure "opened the way to the surge of rearmament among the European Powers which signaled the approach of the Second World War."[32]

This disarmament fiasco occurred at the same time as the occurrence of another major failure. In 1931, Japan began taking over Manchuria in an aggression that eventually resulted in the deaths of many millions of Chinese. When the League's Council, after much delay, finally issued its report, it endorsed the Chinese position. But that was as far as it went. "There was no suggestion of economic or military measures to expel the Japanese," because "none of the great Powers . . . was prepared for drastic action of that kind, despite the challenge to the whole international order implicit in Japan's strategy in Manchuria."[33]

This failure to stop Japan's aggression was "almost a fatal blow" to the League. The truly fatal blow occurred in 1935, after Mussolini's Italy invaded Ethiopia—then called Abyssinia—which was a member of the League. Besides the fact that the League refused to use force or even significant economic sanctions to force Italy to withdraw, its two most powerful members—Britain and France—came up with the notorious Hoare-Laval plan, according to which more than half of Abyssinia would be awarded to Italy. After a public outcry forced the plan's withdrawal, Mussolini simply took the entire nation.

> Abyssinia passed into the Duce's empire and the League's first and final experiment in the enforcement of international law was brought to a close.[34]

After this disaster, the League was simply ignored in 1938–1939, when Hitler began his aggression against Czechoslovakia, Austria, and Poland, thereby provoking World War II.[35]

4

The United Nations
and Its Failure

Acording to F.S. Northedge, although human weakness certainly played a role in the League of Nations' failure, the main problem was "a fatal drawback in the League system" itself—"an inconsistency between the theory of collective security and the necessities of action in the anarchical international system."[1]

Proposals to Overcome Global Anarchy

This realization led many thinkers to propose the creation of an organization that would truly overcome this system.

G. Lowes Dickinson

Perhaps the best-known book of this type was G. Lowes Dickinson's 1926 book, *The International Anarchy, 1904–14*, which made the phrase "international anarchy" famous.[2] Rather than focusing on the particular causes of particular wars, Dickinson said, we need to focus on the underlying cause of all wars, which is international anarchy. It is a mistake to believe that war is inevitable, but "whenever and wherever the anarchy of armed States exists, war does become inevitable."[3]

Accepting the continuation of this conditional inevitability was no longer tenable, Dickinson further argued, because the technology of warfare had become so destructive. Although civilization had thus far survived war, "survival cannot be counted upon in the future." (This was written, it should be noted, two decades prior to the invention of atomic weapons.)[4]

Given these analyses of the problem of war and its seriousness, Dickinson said:

> The way to salvation is the development of the League of Nations into a true international organ to control, in the interests of peace, the policies of all States. . . . The legal openings left for war must be closed. . . . There must be, by consequence, a complete apparatus for the peaceable settlement of all disputes. . . . There must be arrangements for an equitable distribution of important raw materials. . . . And, above all, there must be general, all-round disarmament.[5]

One major problem, of course, was that neither the British empire, to which Dickinson belonged, nor the emerging American empire wanted an "equitable distribution of important raw materials." One of the main purposes of imperialism, of course, has been to garner the lion's share of these materials. Would either the British or the Americans be willing to give up this goal for the sake of merely saving civilization—even after atomic weapons had been invented and used?

Frederick Schuman and Georg Schwarzenberger

In *International Politics* (1933), a very successful international relations textbook, Frederick Schuman argued that war could not be eliminated by attempts at disarmament, arbitration, adjudication, conciliation, or collective security. Schuman was a member of the school of thought known as Political Realism, which emphasizes international anarchy as the underlying cause of war. Although most Realists have followed Hobbes in rejecting a call for global government to overcome war, Schuman argued for overcoming "the Western state system" through the political unification of the world by means of a world federation.[6]

Another major Political Realist who argued this case was Georg Schwarzenberger. In a 1941 book, *Power Politics*, he said that because "power politics, international anarchy and war are inseparable," the "antidote [to war] is international government." By an international government[7] he meant a "world State," preferably of the federal type.[8] Unfortunately, those constructing the United Nations ignored the wisdom of Schuman and Schwarzenberger.

A Widespread Consensus

Many additional illustrations could be given. But, more important than the thought of individual thinkers was the growth of a widespread consensus, after the outbreak of a second world war, that an organization much more powerful than the League needed to be created. In fact, said Robert Hilderbrand in his great book on the origins of the United Nations, the League was "perceived to have failed [so fully] ... that its main role ... was to serve as an example of what the new organization ought not to do."[9] In particular, said F. S. Northedge, "there was a general agreement that the League had failed because it lacked 'teeth.' .... The new world organisation would need to be created on vastly different lines."[10]

Creating such a vastly different organization was, moreover, widely taken to mean one that would, finally, overcome the international anarchy. In Northedge's words:

> The League was decidedly not a super-state, and it was
> for this reason that, in 1944, when the United Nations
> forces allied in defeating the Axis powers met . . . to plan
> a successor to the League, the idea which inspired them
> was that the League had failed *because* it was not a super-
> state, and that something like a super-state would have to
> be created if aggressor states as strong as Nazi Germany
> were going to be halted in their tracks in future.[11]

This intention to create such an organization really did exist. "As originally developed in each of the Big Four nations," wrote Hilderbrand, "the dream that led to the creation of [the United Nations] was a vision of lasting peace."[12]

While World War II was still going on, the US State Department was already involved in intense planning for the postwar world. A central part of this planning involved an idea for an organization that eventually came to be known as the United Nations Organization (now usually known simply as the United Nations, or UN). As originally conceived, it was to be an organization to maintain peace. This organization, since its founding in 1945, obviously has not done this.

Criticism of the UN as an ineffective organization has been common in the United States, especially so in recent years. Most of this criticism implies that the problem is rooted in the UN's personnel—that they are failing to apply the resources at their disposal effectively. The UN's ineffectiveness in maintaining peace and curtailing imperialism is rooted, however, primarily in the UN charter. It is ineffective primarily because it was intended to be so by its architects, the primary architect having been the United States itself.

To understand why the United Nations has been a failure with regard to its primary stated purpose—"to save succeeding generations from the scourge of war"[13]—and hence why the creation of the UN was a missed opportunity of tragic proportions, it is necessary to understand the main issues in the history of the discussion that led up to this failure.

The Failure of the UN

The United Nations has not, of course, brought lasting peace. Indeed, wrote Northedge in 1986, "the United Nations is almost as much a lost cause [with regard to the maintenance of peace] as the League was in the late 1930s."[14] Why? Because, said Hilderbrand, "the final plans for the [United Nations] made a stronger UN impossible by vitiating the strongest features of the Great Powers' original ideas."[15] And why did this change occur?

> The United States, Great Britain, and the Soviet Union decided that their own, individual interests were too important to entrust to a world body, that the wartime dream of an international peacekeeping agency might interfere with their own nationalistic dreams of hegemony. . . . As the postwar period drew nearer, other concerns, especially the protection of their own sovereignty and freedom of action, seemed more important to them than permanent peace.[16]

Emphasizing the central point, Hilderbrand wrote: "At the heart of the new organization's political difficulties lay the expansive postwar ambitions of the Great powers themselves."[17] For example, the United States wanted to be able to "take over strategic islands and bases in the Pacific," while "Stalin viewed a Soviet-led Communist hegemony in Eastern Europe as his most important postwar objective."[18] In short,

> the Big Three saw the defense of their own security, the protection of their own interests, and the enjoyment of the fruits of their victory in the world war as more important than the creation of an international organization to maintain future world peace.[19]

The importance of Hilderbrand's answer cannot be exaggerated. The world since 1945 has suffered the wars in Korea, Vietnam, Nicaragua, El Salvador, the Balkans, Iraq, Syria, the ongoing deadly struggles in Israel-Palestine and elsewhere, and the coups and massacres in Iran, Nicaragua, Chile, Greece, Rwanda, and elsewhere, not because the leaders of the Great Powers discovered that maintaining peace would be impossible. It was because they, just like the princes at the time of Penn, Rousseau, and Kant, did not *want* peace badly enough to give up their "freedom of action" and their "dreams of hegemony."

One implication of Hilderbrand's answer is that most criticisms of the United Nations for its irrelevance to issues of war and peace reflect a misunderstanding about what was intended.

> The U.N.'s shortcomings did not develop out of a failure of application; they were an intentional part of the plans for the world body as negotiated by the Great Powers in the summer of 1944.[20]

The UN has not been able to maintain peace because it was deliberately denied the power to do this. Hilderbrand wrote his book to explain "how the wartime dream of world peace led to plans for a postwar organization lacking the authority to achieve it."[21]

The Change from Dream to Reality

The writings of Penn, Rousseau, Kant, Lorimer, Oppenheim, Dickinson, Schuman, and Schwarzenberg, especially when taken together, laid out all the elements needed by an organization capable of maintaining peace. It would need executive, legislative, and (mandatory) judicial power; it would need the power to tax and to maintain its own military or police force, so that the nations could disarm. In short, it would need to be a superstate. This was the original dream. However:

As the war moved toward its conclusion, the Great Powers began to wonder if they really wanted to create an organization with so much force. Might it not be employed against them? [So they moved to the idea of] creating a revitalized League of Nations that would be less threatening to the[m].[22]

In reading Hilderbrand's book, one can see that, on issue after issue, the Great Powers, especially the United States, deliberately did everything possible to prevent the United Nations from being anything like a superstate. With regard to the name of the organization, for example, Andrei Gromyko, negotiating for the Soviet Union, "suggested the name 'World Union,'" but this was "far too suggestive of a superstate to suit American tastes."[23]

Rejecting "a worldwide peacekeeping organization based on the equality of all states—a 'Federation of the World'—that could threaten their interests as well as their dominance," the Great Powers, especially the United States, opted for "an organization that they could control, at least where their own vital interests were concerned."[24]

An "organization that they could control" would be one without the features listed above. Powers not given to the United Nations include the following.

1. The United Nations would have no power to tax the citizens of the world.

Rather, it relies on payments from the member states. Accordingly, if the United States, for example, does not like some UN policy, it can withhold payment until the policy is modified. This practice is, to be sure, prohibited by the UN Charter, which says that any nation seriously in arrears will lose its vote in the Assembly. But although the United States has been seriously in arrears, it has never been thus disciplined. Without its own money, the UN has no independence from the most powerful states, especially the United States, which, having by far the largest economy, supplied one-fourth of its budget. The resulting ability of the United States to discipline the UN, rather than being disciplined by it, was articulated by Charles William Maynes, who had been the assistant secretary of state in charge of supervising US policy toward the UN during the Carter administration. The United States, said Maynes, should be a "sympathetic but tough parent . . . towards the United Nations. You don't give this dependent child everything it wants."[25]

2. The founders did not give the United Nations its own police or military force.

The Soviets and many analysts in the Great Britain and the United States believed that the "absence of an international police force was a major reason for [the] downfall of [the] League." But FDR said: "We are not thinking of a superstate with its own police forces and other paraphernalia of coercive power."[26] The UN was not even given the power to order states to provide their fair share of troops for a particular operation. Rather, no state could be forced to provide troops without its consent. The UN, accordingly, can exert only as much military force as member states are willing to provide.

A compromise idea, proposed by the Soviet Union, was for "an international air force to punish aggressor states." Such a force had many attractive features: "it could respond quickly, bringing awesome force to bear against a guilty nation"; it would require relatively few personnel, thereby being less costly and allowing each state to keep most of its troops at home. But America vetoed this idea, too, partly because the Pentagon feared that even it would "pose a threat to American sovereignty and freedom of action."[27]

3. The combination of the first two points meant that the United Nations could not provide security for the various states, hence there was no basis for them to disarm.

Unlike the League, in fact, the UN Charter did not even advocate disarmament as a goal for the future. There was also no mention of regulating either the size of armed forces or the manufacture and sale of arms.[28]

4. The UN has no power to prevent war.

The main weakness that had afflicted the League—its lack of "teeth"—was overcome by the creation of the Security Council, with the power to take military action. Two fateful decisions, however, meant that the Security Council's ability to maintain peace was severely restricted. The first decision was that the Security Council would not have the authority to impose pacific settlements prior to the outbreak of hostilities. The British and the Americans both feared that giving the Council this police function "would turn the organization into something too close to an international superstate."[29]

5. The Great Powers gave themselves veto power.

The second fateful decision about the Security Council involved the most contentious issue of the negotiations, which involved the power of the veto. The paralysis of the League of Nations had been caused in large part, as we saw, by the fact that every nation had veto power. The four Great Powers involved in the founding of the UN did not repeat *this* mistake. But they also did not agree to have all Security Council decisions decided by a majority or even two-thirds of its members. Rather, *the four Great Powers made themselves (along with France*[30]*) permanent members of the Security Council, then gave the veto to all permanent members of the Security Council*—which they could use even when they were parties to a dispute. Those who were against this decision pointed out that it would make the UN impotent in relation to the Great Powers, so that its enforcement could be applied only to lesser powers.[31] But the decision was made anyway—making the UN a useful instrument for Great Power imperialism.

6. There is no legislature empowered to pass laws.

Proposals for a world based on law, rather than force, have always included a global legislature, which could pass laws that all nations would have to obey. However, only the Security Council, which has only seventeen members, was given coercive power. The General Assembly, which has representatives from all countries, cannot pass laws, only "resolutions." And these resolutions are enforced only if the Security Council decides to enforce them.

7. There Is No World Court with Power.

The other major basis for a world of laws has been the idea of a world court with mandatory jurisdiction and enforced edicts. There was a strong push by many of the conferees at the 1945 meeting in San Francisco, where the final charter was worked out, to make the Security Council the executor of the court's decisions. However:

> The conferees [thereby] threatened to replace the political hegemony of the Great Powers with the legal authority of a panel of more or less independent jurists.... Such a provision would render the veto meaningless following a court decision.... In addition, mandatory enforcement of court decisions would give the new organization too much of a supranational aspect, which [Great Britain, the USSR, and the USA] wished to avoid.[32]

Whatever these Great Powers wanted to avoid was avoided. The world court, accordingly, is largely impotent. Its decisions are enforced only when all of the Security Council's permanent members want them enforced, rendering enforcement highly arbitrary.

Conclusion

Through these decisions, the United Nations was given "teeth," but *not* "the kind of teeth required to maintain permanent peace."[33] More generally, the United Nations Organization created at San Francisco was far different from the idea originally espoused. Not because that idea was found to be impractical. Rather, to repeat Hilderbrand's conclusion:

> The United States, Great Britain, and the Soviet Union decided that their own, individual interests were too important to entrust to a world body, that the wartime dream of an international peacekeeping agency might interfere with their own nationalistic dreams of hegemony . . . [which] seemed more important to them than permanent peace.[34]

As Hilderbrand pointed out, the inscription on the mansion at Dumbarton Oaks, where the Big Three worked out the basic ideas for the UN, is *Quod severis metes*: One reaps what one sows.

Because the three Great Powers decided to retain the anarchical order, so as to be able to continue to use their power to advance their individual interests, the world reaped: (1) The Cold War; (2) a nuclear arms race that could easily have resulted in nuclear extinction, and still may; (3) dozens of hot wars, bringing unspeakable suffering in many countries, including Korea, Vietnam, Central America, Serbia, Afghanistan, Iraq, and Syria; (4) the US drive to replace global anarchy with the tyranny of a global empire; (5) a global ecological crisis, especially global climate change which, if it continues, will bring civilization to an end.

With regard to the United States in particular: The formation of the United Nations had virtually no effect on the US habit of intervening in other countries, except that it started doing so more covertly (at least until recently), usually through the Central Intelligence Agency (which was also created at that time). For its large-scale interventions, the US has simply used the UN as a cover. More recently, when the US has been unable get UN authorization, the US has simply gone ahead and done what it wanted without it. In fact, it can even be argued that the United Nations has been an aid to US imperialism: In *Masquerade Peace: America's UN Policy, 1944–1945,* Thomas Campbell argued that the US government's aim was "to make the UN policy cover allied power politics with a Wilsonian coating palatable to the American people" and that, shortly thereafter, the Truman administration used "the United Nations as a mask for building an anti-communist Western entente."[35] In any case, the United Nations, as the United States intended, did nothing to curtail America's drive towards a worldwide empire.

Fortunately, Joseph E. Schwartzberg has shown how the UN could be changed into a framework for global democracy in his book, *Transforming the United Nations System: Design for a Workable World.*[36]

It is surely time, finally, to put into place the one system of world order in which peace and security can be combined with freedom: genuine global democracy.

5

Reinhold Niebuhr on Global Government

Reinhold Niebuhr (1892–1971) was one of America's most influential theologians. Although this chapter is about Niebuhr's thought, not his life, a few salient facts about the latter will be helpful in evaluating the former. The eldest son of a German immigrant who had become a minister in the German Lutheran Church, Niebuhr chose to study for the ministry himself because, he said, his father's life seemed more interesting than that of anyone else.[1]

Niebuhr had a natural aptitude for speaking. His biographer reported, for example, that his performance on behalf of Eden Theological Seminary's debating team against a rival school led to his being almost worshipped thereafter by fellow students.

After his rather poor education in both high school and college (which is what Eden then was), Niebuhr attended Yale Divinity School, writing a B. D. thesis on "The Validity and Certainty of Religious Knowledge" and a M. A. thesis on "The Contribution of Christianity to the Doctrine of Immortality," in which he rejected both the resurrection of the body and the immortality of the soul, saying that Christianity's chief contribution to this issue is "its championing the cause of personality in its unequal struggle with the unappreciative forces of nature."[2]

His M.A. thesis was deemed acceptable to earn a degree. But even if his grades had been good enough, he probably would not have accepted the advice of his major professor, Douglas Clyde Macintosh, to try earn a Ph.D. degree.[3] He had become bored with metaphysical and epistemological questions and was anxious to begin dealing with social and ethical issues. In a sermon preached just before beginning his studies at Yale, he said that, although it is difficult to understood the two natures of Christ, the divine trinity, and the communion of the Holy Spirit, "the moral and social program of Christ can be understood."[4]

His public career began while serving a church in Detroit, during the early years of which he was also traveling widely for his church synod to drum up support among German Americans for American participation in World War I. Niebuhr had in 1916 written critically of patriotism in an essay in *The Atlantic* entitled "The Nation's Crime Against the Individual," saying that the nation "claims a life of eternal significance for ends that have no eternal value." But after 1918, said his biographer, Niebuhr became not simply patriotic but "positively bellicose."[5]

Although conscious of the problem of representing the gospel of the God of love while also serving as a "priest of the great God Mars," and wanting a uniform to show his "double devotion," Niebuhr began the process to become a chaplain (although the war ended before this process could be completed).

Afterwards, however, Niebuhr had a change of heart, thanks to the vindictiveness of the Treaty of Versailles and to the treatment of Germans by the occupying French, which Niebuhr witnessed in a trip to Europe in 1923. During that trip he wrote: "This is as good a time as any to make up my mind that I am done with the war business.... I hope I can make that resolution stick."[6] It would stick, however, only until the next war.

After this period of focus on international concerns, Niebuhr returned to domestic matters, concentrating on the question of how religion—in particular, his version of the Social Gospel—could bring about a transformation in the nature of civilization, which meant, primarily, overcoming capitalism. Believing that this social gospel could be effective only if there were a "potent" Christian church, he set out to "see whether spiritual power cannot be developed squarely upon the basis of modernism."[7]

An observation in the early days of his Detroit ministry was especially prophetic of the strategy he would employ. After hearing the evangelist Billy Sunday, Niebuhr wrote that "religious enthusiasm is produced as much by the personal power of the prophet as by the power of his message."[8] He became, in his biographer's words, "the educated Protestant's Billy Sunday,"[9] throwing himself, body and soul, into his sermons and speeches. Hearing "Reinie" speak, many have testified, was an *event*. The fact that he created a school was probably due as much to "the personal power of the prophet" as it was to the power of his message.

When not giving sermons and speeches and serving on committees, Niebuhr was usually at his typewriter. Looking back late in life, he said of himself, "I had a few thoughts and a tremendous urge to express myself. I spoke and wrote all over the place."[10]

Most of his writings were occasional pieces, but he also began producing books, the first two being *Does Civilization Need Religion?* (1927) and *Leaves from the Notebooks of a Tamed Cynic* (1929). After delivering a sermon at Yale Divinity School, he was offered a position there in Christian ethics. Although he turned down this position—which was subsequently filled by his younger brother, Helmut Richard Niebuhr—he in 1930 accepted an invitation from Union Theological Seminary (which was instigated by one of his ardent supporters, Sherwood Eddy).

Within years of joining Union, where he taught "applied Christianity," he published the book that made him famous, the somewhat Marxian *Moral Man and Immoral Society* (1932), which was followed by *Reflections on the End of an Era* (1934). While being even more Marxian socially, this second book involved a rightward turn theologically—a turn that was continued the next year in *An Interpretation of Christian Ethics* (1935).

An invitation to deliver the Gifford Lectures in Scotland in 1939 and 1940 resulted in Niebuhr's most scholarly and substantial (2-volume) work, on which his reputation as a theologian primarily rests, *The Nature and Destiny of Man.* Niebuhr would remain at Union the rest of his teaching career, declining an offer in 1942—again, after giving a sermon—to move to Harvard University.[11]

In 1948 he had an anti-Soviet essay, "For Peace, We Must Risk War," published in *Time, Life,* and *Reader's Digest,* after earlier that year having had his picture on the cover of the 25th-anniversary issue of *Time* magazine: The erstwhile Marxist had become, in Richard Rovere's later phrase, "the official Establishment theologian."[12]

In 1952, at the age of 59, Niebuhr, who had punished his body mercilessly with frenetic activity and excessive smoking for so many years, suffered a series of strokes, with the result that his public activity had to be greatly curtailed.

Niebuhr initiated a school of thought called "Christian Realism." Although the term referred primarily to a religious and political stance, his position was intended to be realistic philosophically as well.

Niebuhr's Philosophical Realism

Niebuhr's thought was certainly realistic philosophically: The world is real in the fullest sense of the term. The world's reality, however, does not mean its self-sufficiency: It is real as *God's creation.* The world, accordingly, does not constitute our total environment. This "total environment" consists of the creator as well as the creation.[13]

Human experience, therefore, involves a dimension not recognized by materialists, including many Political Realists: an awareness of *norms*, which results from the impingement of God upon human consciousness.[14] On this basis, Niebuhr always insisted that moral realism, which recognizes the power of self-interest, need not and should not mean *cynicism,* which says that human behavior is motivated by nothing but self-interest.

Correlative with this affirmation of an experience of normative values is an affirmation of genuine freedom, which is presupposed by the capacity to respond to norms as lures or final causes. Niebuhr was able philosophically to affirm human freedom in this sense by adopting a position that, unlike materialism, does not reduce the human self to the body but that also, unlike dualism, does not posit an ontologically different kind of soul. At least partly through the influence of the philosophy of Alfred North Whitehead, he described conscious human experience, with its self-determining striving, as differing greatly in degree, but not absolutely in kind, from the entities composing the natural world. In *Moral Man and Immoral Society,* Niebuhr wrote:

> Every type of energy in nature seeks to preserve and perpetuate itself and to gain fulfillment within terms of its unique genius. The energy of human life does not differ in this from the whole world of nature. It differs only in the degree of reason which directs the energy. Reason enables him, within limits, to direct his energy so that it will flow in harmony, and not in conflict, with other life.[15]

Christian Realism

At the heart of Niebuhr's religio-political realism, however, is the insistence that human beings do not use their rational freedom, informed as it is with the knowledge of norms, to promote this harmony. "The basis of Christian realism," said Niebuhr in his 1965 book, *Man's Nature and His Communities*, is "that human nature contains both self-regarding and social impulses and that the former is stronger than the latter."[16]

Human beings use their freedom, accordingly, not to promote harmony but to promote their own self-interest at the expense of the good of others. This feature of human nature is not, furthermore, based simply upon ignorance or contingent social structures, which could be overcome; it is rooted in the very center of the human self. Although we are genuinely free, our sinful self-regard is inevitable.

Divine Power

In some thinkers, such a position would be the prelude to praying for the intervention of supernatural grace, through which alone human sinfulness and its destructive consequences can be overcome. Niebuhr's theism, however, was not supernaturalism: It did not affirm divine omnipotence in the sense of the power to interrupt the normal causal relations of the world. Although belief in miracles had been central to his father's theology, the Yale-educated Niebuhr rejected miracles, regarding both nature and history as closed to supernatural intervention.[17]

He did not, furthermore, regard this feature of our world to be based upon a voluntary self-limitation on God's part, which we might expect to be rescinded some time in the future. In an early statement reflecting upon the creation of the world through a long, slow evolutionary process, Niebuhr said:

> The patience of the creative will is a necessary characteristic rather than a self-imposed restraint. There is a stubborn inertia in every type of reality which offers resistance to each new step in creation, so that an emerging type of reality is always in some sense a compromise between the creative will and the established facts of the concrete world. Whether we view the inorganic world, organic life or the world of personal and moral values, each new type

of reality represents in some sense a defeat of God as well as a revelation of him.[18]

Niebuhr's main concern, of course, was not the "inorganic world" or even "organic life" but "the world of personal and moral values." The central implication that he drew from this doctrine of divine power, in conjunction with his doctrine of sin, is that the institution of war will never be overcome.

Whether Niebuhr's political position is significantly different from that of secular realists in any respect will be examined in the discussion of whether Niebuhr's position is philosophically adequate: Did he articulate a position that could be defended in terms of the philosophical criteria of self-consistency and adequacy to experience?

Bases for a Philosophically Adequate Position

Niebuhr's basic philosophical position, as sketched above, would allow a philosophically adequate position to be developed. In the first place, his doctrine that the self is distinct and yet not ontologically different from its bodily members allows him to do justice to our experience, in which we know ourselves to transcend our bodies while being intimately related to them. This doctrine allowed him consistently to affirm human freedom, thereby avoiding the prevalent self-contradiction, which he criticized, of combining a voluntaristic social philosophy with a deterministic psychology.[19]

In the second place, his position also allowed Niebuhr to avoid supernaturalism, with all of its problems. His view of the mind-body relation provided an analogue in our experience for understanding the God-world relation. He wrote:

> God is certainly in the structures and temporal processes just as the human person is "in" its organism. But both the human and the divine person possess a freedom over and above the processes and structures.[20]

Although this statement shows that Niebuhr affirmed a naturalistic, rather than a supernaturalist, theism, he did in his early writings sometimes use the term "supernaturalism" positively.[21] As he pointed out later, however, this term was misleading, because it suggested "a separate order of existence."[22]

One dimension of traditional supernaturalism was its doctrine of divine immutability and impassibility, according to which the world does not affect God. It was central to Niebuhr's position, by contrast, that the world has meaning precisely because it is taken up into the divine life.

The other major dimension of the classical image of God—as wholly external to the world, rather than being related to it as we are to our bodies—is the idea that God can intervene in the world, supernaturally overriding its causal patterns, which Niebuhr rejected.

It was especially Niebuhr's rejection of this latter aspect of supernaturalism that provided the basis for a theology that could be both self-consistent and adequate to the facts of experience. Thanks to this rejection, his theology avoided contradicting the naturalistic presupposition of modern science, according to which there can be no interruptions of the universal nexus of cause and effect. More particularly, Niebuhr's doctrine of divine power was consistent with the fact that our world has evidently been created through a very long, slow, evolutionary process.

No exception to the denial of supernatural interventions was made with relation to christology: Niebuhr rejected the idea that Jesus' full humanity is compatible with his being unconditioned in any respect, such as in knowledge, saying that "it is not possible for any person to be historical and unconditioned at the same time."[23]

This naturalistic theism also, of course, ruled out the view that miraculous intervention guaranteed the inerrancy of the Bible: Niebuhr explicitly rejected what he called "Bibliolatry," according to which the Bible gives us "the final truth, transcending all finite perspectives and all sinful corruptions."[24]

Most important, Niebuhr's doctrine of divine power allowed him to avoid the two most prevalent ways of (inadequately) responding to the problem of evil: by either denying the reality of evil or appealing to mystery. As Niebuhr saw, the classical traditional doctrine of omnipotence, according to which God is "the actual cause of every concrete reality," is essentially pantheistic, denying the gap between the real and the ideal.[25]

More recent theologians have rejected this all-determining version of classical theism, but without giving up the idea of God's essential omnipotence, by affirming a free-will version of classical theism, according to which God voluntarily refrains from determining all events, allowing all or at least some of them (such as human experiences) to act freely. This position still leaves a problem of evil, because this deity by hypothesis *could* intervene to prevent unspeakable horrors.

In any case, Niebuhr, as indicated above, rejected this view of a "self-imposed restraint" on the part of the divine will. Experience provides no warrant, he said, for "the theory that a good God is in essential control of all the universe's forces." Moreover, he said, "Transcendent purpose and creative will in the universe may be scientifically validated, but do not thereby become the effective cause of every natural phenomenon."[26]

Suggesting that God is related to the world as we are to our bodies, Niebuhr added: "[I]t is to be noted that we are not in complete control of our body. There is a life in our body which the soul does not control though it is in intimate relation to it."[27] We need not suspect, accordingly, that the world's evils betoken divine malevolence, or at least indifference. Thanks to his naturalistic theism, Niebuhr could consistently affirm the reality of evil, thereby keeping the all-important tension between the real and the ideal, while also holding to the unambiguous goodness of God.

For the above reasons, Niebuhr's substantive views about the God-world and self-body relations would have allowed him to defend his theological position philosophically—that is, in terms of its intrinsic reasonableness, rather than by appeal to authority. Indeed, his doctrine of divine power, in conjunction with his correlative rejection of infallible revelation, implied that he could only commend his theology in terms of its intrinsic merits, which is what he did.

Already in his B. D. thesis, he had accepted the contention of the French theologian Auguste Sabatier that biblical criticism and evolutionary naturalism had destroyed "authority religion."[28] Under the influence of his own professor, D. C. Macintosh, who argued that theology must become an "empirical science," Niebuhr accepted at least the proposition that religious belief must be grounded in an analysis of universal human experience, rather than in inherited revelation.[29]

Later, in opposition to Ernst Troeltsch's relativism and Karl Barth's way of responding to it with a revelational "positivism that stands above reason," Niebuhr said that we "can escape relativity and uncertainty only by piling experience upon experience, checking hypothesis against hypothesis."[30] We cannot, contrary to Barthianism, insisted Niebuhr, simply assert the truth of the biblical myth "with no effort to validate Christianity in experience against competition with other religions."[31]

Christian Revelation

Niebuhr's mature position, to be sure, did not involve a rejection of revelation, even a specifically Christian revelation. Although Niebuhr retained his concern with universal human experience, he came to hold that any interpretation of this universal experience requires a principle of interpretation based on special experiences. For example, while conscience, as the sense of being placed under obligation and judged, is universally human, the interpretation of this experience as "a relation between God and man . . . is not possible without the presuppositions of the Biblical faith."[32]

This acceptance of special revelation, meaning one that occurred in a particular historical tradition, did not, however, rule out the reasonableness of the resulting theological position. The test is whether the acceptance of the putative revelation leads to a position that is more adequate than those starting with other presuppositions. For example, referring to the Christian idea that the divine mercy transcends the divine judgment, Niebuhr said that, "once this character of God is apprehended in terms of special revelation, common human experience can validate it."[33] More generally, having said of Christian faith that "it illumines experience and is in turn validated by experience," he said of Christian revelation that "it becomes, once accepted, the basis for a satisfactory total explanation of life."[34]

These statements are in harmony with the definition of revelation given by his brother, H. Richard Niebuhr—"Revelation means this intelligible event which makes all other events intelligible"[35] —which Reinhold was said to have accepted.[36] Directly addressing our question of the rationality of Christian faith, Reinhold wrote: "In the sense that the faith of Biblical religion comprehends the totality of things more completely and adequately than any alternative faith, it may be regarded as rational."[37]

The fact that Niebuhr began with assumptions derived from the biblical tradition, accordingly, did not count against the rationality of his theology. This approach could be criticized as "dogmatic," he pointed out, only on the basis of the illusion that empirical inquiry is possible without presuppositions,[38] and by now philosophers have generally come to agree that empiricism in that old sense *is* an illusion.

The Problem of Consistency and Reason

What we have been examining lies at the heart of the Niebuhrian apologetic method: showing that Christian faith provides "the basis for a satisfactory total explanation of life" while simultaneously arguing that the inadequacies of all rival views provide "the most telling negative proof for the Biblical faith."[39]

Nothing examined thus far counts against the philosophical adequacy of Niebuhr's view, its ability to commend itself in terms of its intrinsic merits, apart from any appeal to authority. There remains, however, one more relevant dimension of Niebuhr's position, and this one does create problems. Niebuhr characteristically—as in the last quotation in the previous paragraph—spoke of the *adequacy* of Christian faith. The criteria for philosophical excellence, however, include *consistency* as well as adequacy. Niebuhr himself used this criterion against others, arguing, for example, that Marxism, in presupposing freedom in its social philosophy while espousing determinism in its psychology, was self-refuting.[40] And yet Niebuhr tended to exempt his own position from this criterion, even making a lack of complete self-consistency a virtue.

Niebuhr decided early on that adequacy and self-consistency are at odds, so that any position that is self-consistent will *ipso facto* be inadequate. Consistency, he said, always obscures facts.[41] A clue to why he thought this is perhaps provided by an early comment: "The intellect is too closely wedded to the senses to be an entirely trustworthy witness to truth."[42]

This comment suggests that Niebuhr might have been led by one or more of the thinkers he had studied, such as Immanuel Kant, Albrecht Ritschl, and Henri Bergson, to believe that intellectual categories are inherently such as to distort the true nature of reality. Intellectual self-consistency, accordingly, far from being a test of truth, would be a sure sign of falsity. This view was suggested by a statement seeming to say that Jesus's view of reality was adequate precisely because of its paradoxical and unphilosophical nature.[43]

In any case, Niebuhr held from beginning to end that reality as such, especially the relation between self and body and that between God and world, is "paradoxical," in the sense that no rationally self-consistent explication can do justice to it.

Myths: Primitive and Permanent

This insistence on the permanently paradoxical nature of reality led to Niebuhr's distinctive position on the question of myth. In contrast to Rudolf Bultmann's call for a complete "demythologizing" of Christian theology, Niebuhr said that we must distinguish between two kinds of myths: primitive and permanent. Some myths reflect a prescientific worldview, implying that the chain of natural causes is sometimes interrupted. Myths of this primitive type are to be completely rejected. Other myths, however, express dimensions of reality to which rational categories cannot do justice. These are permanent myths, being suprascientific rather than prescientific. In fact, besides transcending the categories of modern science, they are even suprarational. Belonging to the category of "permanent myths" are the Christian ideas of creation, sin (the "fall"), salvation, and incarnation.[44]

Opposing Rationality with Organism and Freedom

Niebuhr's position here—that permanently valid aspects of historic Christian doctrines are in principle incapable of being explicated in a self-consistent way—involves the fact that he adopted an unnecessarily restricted view of the nature and capacities of "reason." One of the problems in Niebuhr's thought is that, although this point about the inherent limitations of reason plays an extremely important role, he never provided an extended discussion of reason as such. From various occasional comments, however, we can see that he thought of reason as the capacity to conceive universals, think logically, analyze things, trace causal sequences, and conceptually put things back together. In this process, he held, the organic unities and the freedom are lost, because reason's reassemblage, he insisted, results in purely logical or mechanical relations.[45]

Given this idea of reason, the fact to which it most obviously cannot be adequate is freedom. Scientific reason, looking at human behavior externally, understands it in deterministic categories, Niebuhr said, while philosophical reason deals only with the structure of reality, being thereby unable to deal with our freedom beyond structure.[46] Genuine freedom, Niebuhr concluded, "cannot be conceived in any natural or rational scheme of coherence."[47]

Because the human self or person is an essentially self-determining unity, being transcendent over, as well as intimately involved in, the determinisms of nature, Niebuhr spoke of the concept of personality or the self as a "rational absurdity."[48] Interestingly, Niebuhr also said, with an appeal to Whitehead's philosophy, that determinism is bound to be discredited by philosophic thought itself.[49] This recognition suggests that Niebuhr's conclusion, that rational, philosophical thought will permanently be unable to describe reality without denying freedom, was premature.

In any case, mythological thinking is needed, according to Niebuhr, not only for human selfhood, but even for nature, because there are teleological, organic unities in nature analogous to the human self. "The facts of organic growth can be comprehended and described only by mythically transferring the inner unity of the human consciousness (where unity is directly experienced and apprehended) to the external world."[50] Although this process always involves some primitive myth, Niebuhr added, the concept of nature derived from analogy with our own experience "is permanently valid, since reality is actually organic and not mechanical in its processes."[51]

Although Niebuhr sometimes contrasted the freedom of the self with the determinism of nature, he maintained that the fact that all events have natural causes does not mean that the events are fully explained by those causes. In support of this view, he called upon Whitehead's philosophy again:

> It is advisable to consult a metaphysical account of the temporal and natural process before banishing mystery from the realm of either "creation" or "evolution." In Alfred

Whitehead's memorable volume, *Process and Reality,* he posits God as the "principle of concretion" to account for the fact that no previous cause is an adequate explanation for a subsequent event. These events always reveal a relation to previous causes and sequences, but also novel features for which there is no adequate explanation in the previous stream of events.[52]

By conceiving of nature in these terms, Niebuhr pointed out, we would also be in a better position to do justice to human freedom, because modernity's difficulty here has been based on its underestimation of the problem of freedom and necessity in nature. Understanding the rest of nature by analogy with our own experience, accordingly, provides us with a more adequate view. There is, he said,

> a gain for an adequate cosmology, if man uses concepts in his interpretation of the cosmos which he won first of all in measuring the dimension of his own internal reality. Even nature is better understood if it is measured in a dimension of depth which is initially suggested by the structure of human consciousness.[53]

From a Whiteheadian point of view, this is exactly right. But why should organic concepts be called "mythological" and "rationally absurd" when it is agreed that nature really is organic, that there really is freedom in nature, and that using organic concepts constitutes "a gain for cosmology"—which, after all, is a rational enterprise.

Part of the answer seems to be Niebuhr's acceptance of Bertrand Russell's view that the process of ascribing meaning to external reality, by seeing the world as having "the kind of vital and organic unity the self experiences in its own self-consciousness," is not a rational, but a mythological, process. Niebuhr disagreed, to be sure, with Russell's view that this process is always unwarranted.[54] But that is just the point: Why use the term "mythological," which inevitably suggests—no matter how much one may try to redefine and revalorize it—that the process *is* unwarranted, that it necessarily distorts the true nature of things?

The other part of the answer is, of course, Niebuhr's restricted conception of reason, according to which it will forever be incapable of dealing with organic unities and their freedom. Why, however, should he have retained this conception while at the same time appealing to Whitehead's "metaphysical account," which Whitehead called "the philosophy of organism"? The very purpose of this account was to develop a set of categories that *could* deal with organic unities by showing how to conceive the combination of efficient causation and self-determination that we all presuppose in practice. Rather than using Whitehead's philosophy as an occasion to rethink his views about the capacities of reason, however, Niebuhr used it to support his view that reality is inherently paradoxical.

This usage occurred primarily in relation to the God-world relation. Given the fact that Niebuhr took the relation of the human person or self to its body as the best analogue for the relation of God to the world, it followed that he would also regard the latter relation as beyond rational explication. God's relation to the world, which is characterized by both transcendence and immanence, is called "paradoxical" and "mythical," in contrast with more "rational" views that portray God as either totally transcendent (dualism) or totally immanent (pantheism). Niebuhr said, for example:

> Reason always has difficulty with an adequate view of transcendence and immanence. It inclines either to reduce it to a complete dualism or to a complete monism.... [An adequate religion's] optimism is based upon a faith in a transcendent center of meaning which is ... never exhausted in any concrete historical reality. But though it is not exhausted in any such reality it is incarnated there. Like

the human personality in the human body, it lives in and through the body, but transcends it.[55]

Once again, Niebuhr suggested that "reason" could do better by pointing to Whitehead, saying with reference to the latter's early idea of God: "The faith of religion in both the transcendence and immanence of God is given a new metaphysical validation."[56]

However, Niebuhr henceforth did not lessen his insistence that the relation of God to the world can only be expressed mythically, adding that "every authentic religious myth contains paradoxes of the relation between the finite and the eternal which cannot be completely rationalized."[57] Indeed, Whitehead became important to him as a fellow mythical thinker, as he quoted Whitehead's famous definition of religion in his *Science and the Modern World* (which was written before Whitehead had developed his doctrine of God as a full-fledged actuality):

> Religion is the vision of something which stands beyond, behind, and within, the passing flux of immediate things; something which is real, and yet waiting to be realised; something which is a remote possibility, and yet the greatest of present facts; something that gives meaning to all that passes, and yet eludes apprehension.[58]

Niebuhr then added: "These paradoxes are in the spirit of great religion."[59]

What Niebuhr did not do, even though he referred elsewhere to Whitehead's later thought, was to point out that Whitehead went on to develop a conceptuality intended to be self-consistent as well as adequate to the facts of our experience, to speak of God as both transcendent and immanent.

For example, at the end of *Process and Reality*, Whitehead developed a set of antitheses about God and the world that appear, at first glance, to be contradictory. But this appearance of contradiction was overcome by the fact that the terms "God" and

"the world" in the first and second parts of each antithesis refer to
different aspects of God and the world.[60]

Whitehead, in short, was not willing to rest content with
paradox. Far from leaving the impression that speaking of God
necessarily led one away from a fully rational worldview, Whitehead
concluded that a fully rational view could *only* be achieved by
speaking of God.

Opposing Evil and Coherence

The same contrast occurred with regard to the problem of evil.
Niebuhr, as we saw earlier, rejected the traditional doctrine of
omnipotence, adopting instead the Whiteheadian view that the
world has its own power, which cannot be overridden, so that
the divine "patience" is not merely a self-imposed restraint. That
is arguably the one starting point from which one *can* develop a
self-consistent theodicy, reconciling the perfect goodness of the
creator with the evil of the world.

Niebuhr, however, chose not to stress this point, saying instead
that the evil of the world shows that the universe is not fully
"coherent" or "consistent." What he meant thereby was that, if the
world were fully consistent with its ground, which is the eternal
character and purpose of God, one would need to say either that the
world is totally good or else that God is partly evil.[61] Niebuhr even
supported his own preference for empirical adequacy over rational
consistency by quoting Whitehead's well-known (and overdrawn)
contrast between Christianity and Buddhism:

> Christianity has always been a religion seeking a meta-
> physics in contrast to Buddhism which is a metaphysics
> generating a religion. . . . The defect of a metaphysical
> system is the very fact that it is a neat little system which
> thereby oversimplifies its expression of the world. In respect
> to its treatment of evil, Christianity is therefore less clear
> in its metaphysical idea but more inclusive of the facts.[62]

Niebuhr failed to point out that Whitehead, not thinking that Christians should rest content with this situation, subsequently went on to try to articulate the metaphysics that Christianity has long been seeking, so that we could henceforth have a more fully rational view: one that is "clear in its metaphysical idea" as well as "inclusive of the facts."

By contrast, however, Niebuhr seemingly took pains to make his view seem less rational than it really was. Even though he had a view of both the self-body relation and the God-world relation that *could*, as Whitehead's example shows, have been defended as *more* rational than rival views, Niebuhr chose to remain with a restricted conception of reason according to which his view had to be contrasted with "more rational" views.

This strategy cost him dearly, as numerous critics dismissed him as irrational, obscurantist, and fideistic. One such critic said: "I despise Niebuhr's obscurantism"; another said that his statements about the insufficiency of reason mean an "early abdication of thoughtful effort."[63] Fellow theologian Henry Nelson Wieman charged flatly that Niebuhr rejected reason.[64]

One could, of course, defend Niebuhr against these charges, showing that the appearance of irrationalism is due entirely to Niebuhr's stipulated conception of reason and that, given an expanded understanding of rationality, the above "paradoxes" and "myths" can be regarded as fully rational.

However, part and parcel of developing an acceptable philosophical position is *showing* not merely its adequacy to experience but also its self-consistency. One cannot expect other thinkers to take great pains to discover that, in spite of your protestations to the contrary, your position actually is a rational one. Niebuhr himself certainly did not do this with regard to rival positions, but used apparent inconsistencies in them as reasons to dismiss them.[65] In any case, the first dimension of the philosophical inadequacy of Niebuhr's form of realism is that, by adopting a too restrictive notion of "reason," he unnecessarily portrayed his own position as irrational.

A More Serious Problem of Inconsistency

Whereas the first dimension of Niebuhr's philosophical inadequacy, not consisting of truly substantive problems that would necessitate either inconsistency or inadequacy, could have been easily corrected, a second dimension is more serious. This second dimension is the fact that, in his mature position, Niebuhr adopted positions that truly are problematic, apart from any too restrictive view of reason.

This second dimension may be derivative from the first: That is, perhaps Niebuhr, having long derided the "rational" demand for self-consistency as antithetical to empirical adequacy, became less concerned than in earlier days with the distinction between merely "paradoxical" and truly self-contradictory views. Perhaps, having long held that "religious faith cannot be simply subordinated to reason or made to stand under its judgment," he became less concerned with the accompanying qualification, which he had articulated in NDM I, that "religious faith . . . cannot be in contradiction to reason."[66] In any case, Niebuhr did, in fact, come to adopt rationally inconsistent formulations.

With regard to the doctrine of God's relation to the world, as we saw, Niebuhr adopted a view similar to Whitehead's, perhaps having derived it, in fact, from Whitehead. According to that view, the fact that the world's causal power is never interrupted or overridden, so that each reality represents (in Niebuhr's words) "a defeat as well as a revelation of him" (see page 47 in this chapter) is not due to a divine self-limitation (although Niebuhr would later appeal to the self-limitation view to defend God's goodness).

Rather, according to Whitehead, "creativity," which is the formless stuff embodied in all actualities, is inherent in finitude as well as in God. This means, in traditional language, that God did not create the world *ex nihilo,* but by bringing order out of chaos. This creative activity occurs through the presentation of ideal forms, which subsist as pure possibilities in God's nature. In his early thinking, Niebuhr seemed to adopt this view, saying that creation "out of nothing" means only that the creative source of novelty lies beyond that which we can see; and he spoke of the possibilities of creation out of "things that are not,"[67] which seem to be the Whiteheadian ideal forms.

Later, however, Niebuhr extolled the "mythical" or "suprarational" biblical view over against those cosmologies that "are forced to presuppose some unformed stuff, some realm of chaos, which *nous* fashions into order, and to identify this process with creation."[68] The biblical doctrine, he said, "derives both the formless stuff and the forming principle from a more ultimate divine source."[69] The fact that this doctrine is suprarational, he said, "is proved by the fact that, when pressed logically, it leads to the assertion that God creates *ex nihilo*."[70] In line with this thinking, Niebuhr wrote that "an impotent or limited goodness is not divine" and speaks negatively of a "finite God who is frustrated by the inertia of some 'given' stuff of reality."[71]

Niebuhr's later view, according to which God is the source of the formless energy or vitality embodied in all creatures, requires a choice between two options, each of which is problematic. *One option* would be to follow this position to the logical conclusion of creation *ex nihilo*, which would entail that the freedom and causal power possessed by the creatures are wholly derivative from God. This would entail, in turn, that God's failure to intervene supernaturally now and then in the world *is* due to a voluntary self-limitation, which would undermine the basis of Niebuhr's early theodicy. Carrying Niebuhr's later doctrine of God to its logical conclusions would, furthermore, undermine the basis for his religio-political realism, which presupposes that God cannot overcome human sin in history. The doctrine of creation *ex nihilo* would imply that God *could* do so but chose not to do so—which, in the light of the nuclear and ecological threats, would give Niebuhrian realism an even worse problem of evil. Finally, this doctrine of creation would imply divine omnipotence in the traditional sense, which, as Niebuhr himself said, results in an essentially pantheistic view, which in turn undermines the most fundamental point of Niebuhr's theological ethic: the tension between the real and the ideal.

There are signs that Niebuhr moved in this direction to an extent, coming to think of history as in some way determined by a "mysterious divine sovereignty."[72] For example, the title of one of his wartime essays, "History (God) Has Overtaken Us,"[73] seems to equate the movement of history—in this case, the Japanese bombing of Pearl Harbor, which brought the United States into the war—with the will of God.

In another essay of the same year (1943), Niebuhr spoke of the "grace that determines the lives of men and nations." If the factors that determine national eminence are purely accidental, he said, "then history itself has no meaning; for in that case it would be the fruit of caprice."[74]

The alternative view, which Niebuhr endorsed, is that evil finally exists "under the dominion of God."[75] Such statements perhaps reflect the views of H. Richard Niebuhr, who had encouraged his elder brother to read Paul, Augustine, Luther, and Calvin, and had confided to him of being himself "a bit pantheistic or better Spinozistic."[76]

Reinhold, however, while having newly incorporated this idea of an all-determining divine providence in some sense, clearly did not make its implications central to his theology. For example, after saying that faith "discerns a mysterious divine sovereignty over the whole drama of human events," he added that this faith "ought not be surprised by any manifestations of evil in history."[77] And, although it was a caricature when Joseph Haroutanian said to Niebuhr that "the 'tension' between the ideal and the real seems to me to be the essence of your religion,"[78] this tension did remain central to him to the end.

Niebuhr could avoid all these unacceptable implications for divine goodness and human ethics only by taking the *second option,* that of simply refusing to carry through his position to its logical conclusion. Besides retaining the tension between the ideal and the real, Niebuhr continued, for the most part, to define divine "omnipotence" in terms not of God's power to determine history, but of God's power "beyond history." For example, in the same book in which he had ridiculed "a finite God who is frustrated by the inertia of some 'given' stuff of reality," he also said that some created forms of life are "so independent that even the power of God, acting merely as power, cannot reach the final source of their defiance."[79] With regard to omnipotence, he said:

> The problem of history . . . is not that God should be revealed as strong enough to overcome the defiance of the evil against His will, but as having resources of mercy great enough to redeem as well as judge all men. . . . The final majesty of God is contained not so much in His power within the structures as in the power of His freedom over the structures.[80]

However, taking this second option, which means refusing to be responsible for the logical conclusions of one's position, was to reject reason in the most fundamental sense of the word. It was to make faith "contrary to reason," which Niebuhr himself said should not be done. But this is, in effect, what he did.

Another problem of self-consistency arose with regard to another aspect in which Niebuhr moved back toward the traditional doctrine of God. The issue involved is the idea, referred to above, that the meaning of life and history lies "beyond history." The import of this statement is that the world is taken up into God. In contrast with the traditional view that God is immutable and impassible in all respects, unable to be affected by the creatures, Niebuhr held, with Whitehead and Charles Hartshorne, that God not only suffers with the world but also takes all of its occurrences into the divine life, thereby giving them a permanent meaning. Niebuhr even cited Hartshorne in this regard, endorsing the latter's view, according to which (in Niebuhr's words):

> God's perfection must be defined primarily in terms of His capacity for self-transcendence rather than in the traditional concepts of omnipotence, if the Christian doctrine of His ability to enter into loving relationships with suffering men is to have any meaning.[81]

Whitehead called this aspect of God, in which the world contributes to the divine experience, the "consequent nature" of God (in contrast with the "primordial nature," which contains and supplies the ideal forms); Hartshorne called this aspect God's "concrete states" (in contrast with God's "abstract essence"). In spite of their differing terminologies, however, Whitehead and Hartshorne were at one in insisting that this aspect of God—which is really God as a whole, God as fully actual—is *temporal*, in contrast with the other aspect of God, which is eternal in the sense of nontemporal. For Whitehead and Hartshorne, the traditional idea that God is immutable and impassible in all respects is part and parcel of the objectionable idea that God is eternal in all respects, rather than being, like the world, in process.

From their viewpoint, God does not know the future. God's "omniscience," Hartshorne said, means that God at any time knows *all things that are then knowable.* This category, however, does not include "future events," because they do not yet exist, and what they *will* be has not yet been decided. In contrast with traditional theism, which said that God knows the whole history of the universe in one simultaneous glance, as it were, the "process theism" of Whitehead and Hartshorne thinks of God's knowledge of the world in temporal terms.

Niebuhr, however, combined his central assertion, that history is meaningful because it is taken up into God, with the traditional notion of a divine "total simultaneity." He said:

> The "partial simultaneity" of man by which he comprehends the sequences of time into his consciousness inevitably carries with it, by way of implication, a sense of a divine "total simultaneity" which comprehends the sequences of time beyond man's own capacity of comprehension. A suprahistorical eternity is implied in history because the capacity by which man transcends temporal sequences . . . implies a capacity of transcendence which is not limited by that sequence.[82]

Niebuhr evidently thought that this doctrine, far from threatening his affirmation of the meaningfulness of historical existence, undergirded it. He wrote:

> The divine consciousness gives meaning to the mere succession of natural events by comprehending them simultaneously, even as human consciousness gives meaning to segments of natural sequence by comprehending them simultaneously in memory and foresight.[83]

However, this idea would imply that, in Franklin Gamwell's words, "Niebuhr understands transcendent reality to be without unrealized states of affairs," so that "the Kingdom of God is, always has been, and always will be transcendently realized."[84] As Gamwell argued, moreover, this idea implicitly contradicts the assumption, which Niebuhr regarded as crucial for an ethic of historical responsibility, that our actions in history are of ultimate importance. If, for God, all values are eternally realized, the idea that we are making a contribution of ultimate significance is an illusion. Niebuhr's ethic was contradicted by his theism.

Still another inconsistency that does not depend upon Niebuhr's restricted notion of reason involves the doctrine of sin. According to this doctrine, we are sinful at the very core of our beings, but we are responsible for this sinfulness because we are free. We cannot excuse ourselves by claiming that the source of sin lies outside ourselves, whether in God, society, or any historical contingency. Our sinfulness is, furthermore, not necessitated by our finitude; to say that would be to deny the biblical affirmation of the goodness of the creation. Sin "can only be understood as a self-contradiction, made possible by the fact of [our] freedom but not following necessarily from it."[85] We are, accordingly, responsible for our sin. So far so good.

But Niebuhr also, in defending a deliteralized version of the doctrine of original sin, insisted that, although sin is not necessary, it is inevitable.[86] Admitting that this idea is "seemingly absurd," Niebuhr began his discussion with the statement that it is "not easy to state the doctrine of original sin without falling into logical pitfalls."[87]

What we learn, however, is that all the consistent doctrines of sin are inadequate. Even when literalistic ideas of inheritance from a primal ancestor are eliminated, "the doctrine remains absurd from the standpoint of pure rationalism, for it expresses ... a truth which logic cannot contain."[88] This truth is, said Niebuhr, that we sin inevitably, because "sin posits itself,"[89] and yet we are responsible, because we sin freely.

Having said, "Naturally a position which seems so untenable from a logical standpoint has been derided and scorned not only by non-Christian philosophers but by many Christian theologians," Niebuhr then commended "Pascal's frank acceptance of the logical absurdity of the doctrine of original sin."[90] It is surely the case, as Niebuhr said, that "complexity in the facts of experience [should not] be denied for the sake of a premature logical consistency." Moreover, he insisted, "Loyalty to all the facts may require a provisional defiance of logic."[91] It is something else, however, to rest content with such a defiance, thereby making it permanent.

In sum: Niebuhr accepted the idea that a theology's claim to truth must be based on its intrinsic merits, not on an appeal to authority. He adopted a worldview, furthermore, that would have allowed him to articulate a theological position that could be defended in terms of the philosophical criteria of self-consistency and adequacy to experience. He failed, however, in terms of the criterion of self-consistency, partly because he adopted a too restrictive notion of the capacity of reason, and partly because he accepted some traditional theological formulations that, even apart from that restrictive notion of reason, are inconsistent with the remainder of his position.

Niebuhr's Advocacy of Global Government

Although Niebuhr's successes and failures with regard to philosophical adequacy are important, even more important is the question of the political adequacy of his brand of realism. This estimation of relative importance would agree with Niebuhr's own: In his first book, having said that Christianity faced two major challenges—the metaphysical one of reconciling religion with modern science and the ethical one of disproving the charge that religion is socially harmful or at least impotent—he said, with a nod to Whitehead, that the first was being solved. The more difficult and more important task, he said, was the ethical challenge.[92]

Moreover, Niebuhr's main justification for accepting paradoxical doctrines was that they, in his view, were morally more potent than more consistent ideas. Although religion needs a metaphysical basis, Niebuhr said, moral potency is more important than metaphysical consistency.[93] An assessment of his position as philosophically inadequate, accordingly, would have disturbed him less than a negative judgment with regard to its socio-political adequacy.

Religious Realism

In approaching this issue, the most important question is what the word "Christian" or "religious" before "realism" adds. The short answer is that it connotes the reality and efficacy of normative values. Although Joel Rosenthal used his term "righteous realists" to refer to American realists in general (Hans Morgenthau, Walter Lippman, George Kennan, Dean Acheson, and Reinhold Niebuhr), because of their concern to reconcile morality and power,[94] this term would apply preeminently to Niebuhr.

A less colorful but more illuminating term for his position would be "idealistic realism": He insisted that politics is the realm of "moral ambiguity," not, as Hans Morgenthau said, "amorality."[95] Against the tendency of Political Realism to degenerate into cynicism, Niebuhr always insisted that ideals are real and that they have a real, if limited, efficacy on human experience and behavior.

The basic question of this section is the extent of the limits placed upon this efficacy, especially with reference to the possibility of creating a structure for global governance that would put an end to the war-system and provide a framework for dealing with other questions vital to the sustainability of human civilization.

Before turning to that question, however, we need to consider more completely the factors in the Christian worldview articulated in Niebuhr's early books, in which he expressed his desire to show the social relevance and potency of Christian faith, which would make a *religious* realism based thereon markedly different from secular Political Realism.

The most important factor in Niebuhr's outlook, making it distinctively religious, of course, was his doctrine of God. The reality and power of God explained how ideals become effective in human experience: The "impingement of God" upon human consciousness explains *why* we experience a tension between the real and the ideal.[96]

The specifically biblical idea of the world as God's creation, furthermore, says that the world is essentially *good,* in contrast with Manichean views, which see the world as essentially evil. This twofold idea, that the world is good and its good Creator is active within it, provides a basis for *hope*, a reason to believe that things can be better.

Of course, in rejecting divine omnipotence, Niebuhr rejected the idea that God could *unilaterally* bring about a better world. But precisely this denial protects the distinction between the real and the ideal. Also, in removing the basis for complacency provided by classical theism, this rejection of divine omnipotence supported William James's "strenuous mood."

The belief that God is acting in the world in terms of ideals provided, furthermore, an explanation for the novelty that has already appeared in the world and the basis for expecting God to bring forth further novelty, so that we do not have to think of history as perennially the same. Still more, thinking in terms of the Creator of the world provided a basis for thinking not only about immediate problems but also trying to imagine the world from the divine standpoint, thereby to think in terms of the long-run good of the planet.

With regard to christology, Niebuhr had inherited the perspective of the Social Gospel, which emphasized not the metaphysical christology of Nicaea, or even the picture of Jesus as the Christ portrayed by John and Paul, but the Jesus of the synoptic gospels as reconstructed by the quest for the historical Jesus—the Jesus who proclaimed not himself but the coming reign of God, in which the war, injustice, and inequality of the present time would be overcome. The will of God, for the young Niebuhr as for other Social Gospelers, was understood to be the reign of God on earth. This liberal Christian version of theism, accordingly, provided both hope and religious motivation for striving to bring about an end to those structures that were blocking the creation of a just society—which at that time for Niebuhr were primarily capitalism and international anarchy.

Also important is the fact that, as a Christian theologian instead of simply a free-floating social reformer, Niebuhr potentially had a very large grassroots organization as a social basis for his envisaged reforms. If he could persuade and inspire the Christian church to adopt these reforms as embodiments of the divine will for the present time and thereby as its own mission, the potential for change was tremendous. By contrast, most would-be social reformers are markedly *unrealistic* in the sense that, having no social basis, they have virtually no chance for success. Niebuhr, like the advocates of the Social Gospel in general, had a potential ready-made organization with millions of members around the world, if only he could inspire them. They were already committed to serving the will of God; he had only to convince them that at the center of the divine will at the present time must be the overcoming of capitalism and the war-system.

Niebuhr's Advocacy of World Government

Apart from registering the fact that the replacement of capitalism by socialism was a central part of Niebuhr's early agenda, this chapter will henceforth not deal with the issue of socialism vs. capitalism, except incidentally, focusing instead only on the issue of international anarchy and war.

Indeed, Niebuhr did come for a time, during the height of World War II, to regard the task of overcoming international anarchy as paramount. In spite of his resolution, expressed after the first world war, to be "done with the war business," he campaigned vigorously for the American entry into World War II.

In fact, he had hoped that his 1940 volume of essays, *Christianity and Power Politics,* would become one of the key weapons for the cause of intervention. However, although it provoked an uproar in the Protestant press, especially among pacifists, it was ignored by the secular press.[97]

Moreover, his second series of Gifford Lectures were less than sterling, as his heart was instead in the war effort. However, while the lectures were not terribly good, the resulting second volume of *The Nature and Destiny of Man* turned out to be, arguably, Niebuhr's best book: Thanks to the entry of the United States into the war following the bombing of Pearl Harbor, Niebuhr could now, as his biographer put it, "take time" for the book.[98] As Niebuhr indicated in the aforementioned essay "History (God) Has Overtaken Us," all his activity probably counted for nought: "For years we argued whether or not we should go to war," wrote Niebuhr. "Then history descended upon us and took the decision out of our hands."[99]

The book was also better than most of his other books thanks to the labors of Ursula Niebuhr (his wife) and several friends, including Henry Sloane Coffin (the president of Union Theological Seminary), who helped with the rewriting.[100]

However, Niebuhr's fervent belief that America should get involved in this war, once it had begun, betokened no fondness for war as such. And the horrors of this war surely greatly increased his conviction that we need a new world order in which war would be precluded. In any case, it was in 1943, in *Human Destiny* (the second volume of *The Nature and Destiny of Man*) that he published his most passionate statements about the need for some form of world government.

To those who know the later Niebuhr as an implacable foe of world government, the fact and the force of his argument may be surprising. In a section on "Justice and World Community," Niebuhr spoke of the possibility and necessity of "enlarging the human community so that the principle of order and justice will govern the international as well as the national community." He then added that "our civilization is undone if we cannot overcome the anarchy in which nations live."[101]

In a later section, after saying that there is nothing inevitable about the emergence of a world government, as shown by the fact that the greater intimacy created by modern technical civilization prompts world wars instead of mutual sharing, he wrote that we are now "under the obligation of elaborating political instruments which will make such new intimacy and interdependence sufferable." Our "very survival," he added, is dependent upon it.[102]

He wrote even more forcibly about this need in occasional pieces. In "American Power and World Responsibility," he said that, in this period of world history, "the paramount problem is the creation of some kind of world community" through which the world can "find a way of avoiding complete anarchy in its international life."[103] A section entitled "Most Urgent Problem" began: "The world's most urgent problem is the establishment of a tolerable system of mutual security for the avoidance of international anarchy," after which he gave this prediction: "This will be the great battle of the next decades."[104] In another essay of the same year, he wrote: "It [the world] must escape international anarchy or perish."[105]

He even, using language reminiscent of his more Marxist period, spoke of "the irrefutable logic of history." "This logic is irrefutable," he stated, "because an economically interdependent world must in some sense become a politically integrated world community or allow potential instruments of community to become instruments of mutual annihilation."[106] These statements, it should be emphasized, were all written prior to the development of nuclear weapons.

For most of his life, Niebuhr held that, as bad as war is, tyranny is even worse. But that conviction did not detract from the perceived importance of overcoming anarchy because, he said, "Nazi tyranny grew on the soil of our general international anarchy."[107] International anarchy, in other words, is the precondition for tyranny as well as for war. In our concern to overcome anarchy, however, we must not create the conditions for a more sweeping tyranny.

Niebuhr's treatment of this dual problem is one of the places in which his blend of idealism and realism appeared. Idealists, while appreciating the danger of anarchy, have usually not sufficiently feared the perils of tyranny that a powerful government creates. But realists, who focus on this perennial problem to the neglect of the perils or anarchy, have also failed to appreciate the novelty of the present situation, in which the peril is greater than ever before. What is needed is a way to avoid both anarchy *and* tyranny.[108]

With respect to this twofold task, Niebuhr was clear about the requirements for avoiding anarchy.

> There must be an organizing centre [which can] arbitrate conflicts from a more impartial perspective than is available to any party of a given conflict; . . . it must coerce submission to the social process by superior power whenever the instruments of arbitrating and composing conflict do not suffice; and finally it must seek to redress the disproportions of power by conscious shifts of the balances whenever they make for injustice.[109]

Niebuhr explained the necessity for "superior power" by reference to his doctrine of human nature. The unity of vitality and reason in human nature, he said,

> guarantees that egoistic purposes will be pursued with all vital resources which an individual or collective will may control. Therefore social restraints upon these anti-social purposes must be equally armed with all available resources.[110]

A realistic view of human nature, in other words, dictates that a world governing body, to be effective, must have sufficient power to force compliance. On this basis, Niebuhr in 1945 described as "unbelievably naive" those interpreters of the charter for the United Nations who failed to understand that "no foundation for an international security system had been laid."[111]

Besides having superior force, the central organizing body would also, as the above quotation indicates, need to have an "impartial perspective." Already in 1928, Niebuhr had said, with reference to international conflict: "If there is any possibility of force being redemptive, it is an absolute prerequisite that it be exerted by an agency that is impartial."[112]

With regard to the nature of an international agency that would be both impartial and precluded from degenerating into a tyranny, Niebuhr was less explicit. His general answer to the threat of tyranny, however, was *democracy*, with its various checks and balances against the accumulation of power in any one branch of government.[113] The implication of Niebuhr's overall position, accordingly, was that the international governing body would need to be a global democracy. In fact, having said that "order is the first purpose of the international, as of every other, community," he said: "Democracy is an ideal form of such order."[114] We will return to this issue below. For now, there is another dimension of Niebuhr's view of democracy to examine.

As we saw in Chapter 2, the main reason why most Political Realists have ignored or even ridiculed the idea of global government is the conviction that it is impossible. By holding a more idealistic version of realism, however, Niebuhr thought otherwise. His more idealistic version consisted in holding that, while human selfishness must always be protected against, the achievements of democratic societies refute the completely pessimistic view of Hobbes and Luther, from which it would follow that conflicts of self-interest must always be settled by force: "The capacity of communities to synthesize divergent approaches to a common problem and to arrive at a tolerably just solution proves man's capacity to consider interests other than his own."[115]

The last part of that quotation suggests one of Niebuhr's most famous statements, published in a 1944 book in which he succinctly summarized the argument of his idealistic realism, or realistic idealism, for the possibility and the necessity of democracy: "Man's capacity for justice makes democracy possible; but man's inclination to injustice makes democracy necessary."[116] The latter part of this statement rules out an absolute monarchy: The failure of monarchists such as Hobbes and Luther is that they did not apply their generally pessimistic analysis of human nature to the ruler, whose own inclination to injustice gets inflated with absolute power. The former part of the statement is, obviously, aimed at the assumption of the too-pessimistic realists that human beings are incapable of democratic self-rule.

What has not generally been recognized, however, is that Niebuhr's statement, at least when he first published it, was meant in part to support *the possibility as well as the necessity for democracy at the global level.*

That this is so can be seen by examining the book's title essay, "The Children of Light and the Children of Darkness," in which the statement appeared. Niebuhr defined the "children of light" as those "who believe that self-interest should be brought under the discipline of a higher law" for the sake of the community as a whole. The "children of darkness" are "the moral cynics, who know no law beyond their will and interest." These definitions are justified, Niebuhr said, because "evil is always the assertion of some self-interest without regard to the whole," whereas the good is "always the harmony of the whole on various levels."[117]

Given these definitions, Niebuhr clearly identified with the children of light, who are idealistic realists, overagainst the pure (cynical) realists. But his criticism was also directed against the "*foolish* children of light," who have "underestimated the power of self-interest, both individual and collective."[118] Because of this error, they were confident "of achieving an *easy* resolution of the tension and conflict between self-interest and the general interest,"[119] because they "believed that it was possible to achieve an *uncontrolled* harmony" among the nations.[120]

The implication is that a *wise* (realistic) idealism would take on the *difficult* task of working for a *controlled* harmony. "Modern democratic civilization" has been "sentimental," said Niebuhr, because it "has an *easy* solution for the problem of anarchy and chaos on both the national and international level of community, because of its fatuous and superficial view of man."[121]

In the final section of the essay, Niebuhr said that democratic theory has been "just as stupid in analyzing the relation between the national and international community as in seeking a too simple harmony between the individual and the national community."[122] With regard to Hegel, Niebuhr said that "he saw little possibility of constructing a legal structure of universal proportions which might guard the interests of the universal community." Hegel, therefore, "tended to regard the demands of the state as final because he saw no way of achieving a legal or political implementation of the inchoate community which lies beyond the state."[123] Hegel's was, accordingly, a "sentimental doctrine," because he imagined that the nation, while being *politically* autonomous, would be *morally* bound to the welfare of humanity as such.[124]

In sum: Although Niebuhr's call for world government in this essay is much more muted—so much so that many readers have evidently missed it—we can, by reading it in the light of other writings of the same period, see that it was saying that a democratic government at the supranational level is both a necessity and a possibility—albeit not an *easy* possibility. For example, in a statement from one of those other essays about order at the international level, which was only partially quoted above, Niebuhr wrote: "Democracy is an ideal form of such order, and is not easily established."[125]

While believing that global government was both necessary and possible in principle, Niebuhr's realism also led him to say, in "American Power and World Responsibility," that the "world problem cannot be solved if America does not accept its full share of responsibility for solving it."[126] This stance meant, in turn, that the church, especially in the United States, had a crucial role to play. Having said that "America must not fail," Niebuhr added, in reference to the Federal Council of Churches: "We must find a way of placing the power of America behind the task of world order."[127]

Niebuhr thought, in fact, that anyone viewing the new global situation in the light of Christian faith should conclude this to be the church's *primary* task of our time: Having said in "Plans for World Reorganization" that a "profound Christian faith . . . hears the divine command in every new historical situation," he added: "The Christian ought to know that the creation of some form of world community, compatible with the necessities of a technical age, is the most compelling command of our day."[128] Emphasizing how crucial the church's "prophetic mission" was, Niebuhr said: "If the nations should fail . . . the failure would be the consequence of the prior failure of the Christian church."[129]

The idea that overcoming international anarchy by the creation of a global democracy was the divine will was also expressed by Niebuhr in a negative way. In a 1937 essay entitled "Do the State and Nation Belong to God or the Devil?" he wrote:

> The nation is as much the servant of the devil as the servant of God. The nation may be the incarnation of the principle of order within the community, but it is also the incarnation of the principle of anarchy between communities.[130]

If the demonic is that which is diametrically opposed to the divine, and if international anarchy in our time has become demonic, then it follows that devotion to the divine purpose entails overcoming this anarchy. Insofar as it belongs to the Church's very *raison d'être* to represent the divine point of view as best it can, the Church should be trying to move the nations in this direction.

Niebuhr Fails to Give Full-Fledged Support to Global Democracy

Although Niebuhr gave theological support to the cause of

overcoming international anarchy in these ways, his thinking contained yet another potential theological support, which he, because of his realism, could not develop. The idea in question arose in his analysis of the idea of a Messiah, in the sense of an ideal ruler who would bring justice and peace. In the ethical-universalistic type of Messianism, Niebuhr said:

> The momentary triumph of evil in history is seen as a threat to the meaningfulness of history and this threat is overcome by the hope of the coming of a Messianic king, who will combine power and goodness.[131]

This idea is mythical, however, because "only God can perfectly combine power and goodness"; the expectation of an ideal king "hopes for an impossible combination of the divine and the historical."[132] Niebuhr believed that, although it is possible for some individuals *in contemplation* to rise to a high level of impartiality or disinterestedness, this is not possible for any self *in action*—one who is actually participating in history, with its claims and counterclaims.[133]

> For there is no self in history or society, no matter how impartial its perspective upon the competitions of life, which can rise to the position of a disinterested participation in those rivalries and competitions.[134]

This impossibility of "the perfect coincidence of power and goodness" in any finite individual led to Niebuhr's distinctive christological claim: "It is impossible to symbolize the divine goodness in history in any other way than by complete powerlessness, or rather by a consistent refusal to use power in the rivalries of history."[135]

This claim is combined with another, which is that Messianism, even of the ethical-universalistic type, is surpassed in profundity by biblical "prophetism." This more profound perspective, which alone was based on genuine revelation, involves the prophetic perspective. It sees that "the consummation of history cannot be a Messianic reign . . . which resolves the conflicts of history in a reign of peace," but can only be in a divine mercy beyond history.[136]

However, given Niebuhr's (1) insistence on the necessity of world government, (2) his insight that such a government could bring justice and peace only if it employed its power from an impartial perspective, which is concerned with the good of the whole human community, and (3) his insistence that democratic representation is the only way to approach that kind of impartiality, one might well have expected Niebuhr's analysis to conclude quite differently. Having said that the idea of an "ideal king" is mythical, because no finite individual could be trusted to wield overwhelming power impartially, Niebuhr might have said that it nevertheless points to a real possibility, which can now be actualized: a global democratic government.

Although such an organization, being made of morally flawed as well as intellectually limited human beings, would not by any means *perfectly* incarnate the divine coincidence of power, wisdom, and goodness, it would allow the closest approximation possible— perhaps close enough to bring about a peaceable, sustainable, and increasingly just mode of human civilization.

Why did not Niebuhr develop this line, which would have seemed the natural one, given the development of his thought as summarized above? The reason was evidently his acceptance of a dictum of modern Political Realism, which is most clearly expressed in the essay entitled "Plans for World Reorganization" (which is the essay calling this task "the most compelling command of our day"). In this essay, Niebuhr contrasted the ideas of the idealists and the realists (whom he also calls "the historical school" or "the historical realists"). Whereas the idealists rightly stress the novel element in our situation and the need for justice, their ideal scenarios fail to take account of the realities of power. The realists, by contrast, may ignore the issue of justice and may, by focusing upon perennial factors, fail to recognize the novelty and hence urgency of our situation; but the realists did understand the issue of power:

> The historical realists know that history is not a simple rational process but a vital one. All human societies are organizations of diverse vitalities and interests by power. Some dominant power lies at the center of every social organization. Some balance of power is the basis of whatever justice is achieved in human relations.[137]

Not understanding this, but viewing history from a purely rational, moral perspective, the idealists call for a "federation of the world."

> They think of such a federation not primarily in terms of the complex economic and social interests and vitalities, which must be brought into and held in a tolerable equilibrium. Least of all do they think of the necessity of some dominant force or power as the organizing center of the equilibrium.[138]

Even those idealists who are conscious of the problem of power "deal with it abstractly," said Niebuhr:

> They project some central pool of power without asking what tributaries are to fill the pool. . . . They conceive of some federation of the world with an international police force, and with a newly and abstractly created moral and political prestige, sufficient to maintain itself against the divisive forces that will inevitably challenge its authority.[139]

They assume, in other words, that the powerful nations would, by seeing the necessity for a global democracy in which all nations are equal, give up their national sovereignty and their power to shape the world to their advantage.

Rejecting "these illusions of the rationalists and idealists," Niebuhr said that "the task of world organization must be attempted from the standpoint of the historical realism."[140] The two main groups within this school were the balance-of-power realists and the imperialistic realists. The former group rejects the idea of an international political organization, saying that we need only to reconstruct the balance of power. Niebuhr dismissed this approach because "an unorganized balance of power is potential anarchy and cannot preserve peace."[141]

Niebuhr endorsed instead the approach of the other group, which "believes in some kind of imperial organization of the world, with some small group of dominant nations furnishing the imperial power."[142] This group was more fully realistic:

> They know that a balance of power must be organized and that a dominant power must be the organizing center. They expect either America, or the Anglo-Saxon hegemony, or the four great powers, Russia, China, Britain, and America, to form the organizing center of the world community. I think they are right in this thesis and that there is no possibility of organizing the world at all that will not be exposed to the charge of "imperialism" by the idealists who do not take the problem of power seriously.[143]

However, the idea of a world government with "an implied hegemony of the stronger powers," which Niebuhr endorsed as "inevitable"—in spite of its inherent "peril of a new imperialism"[144]—was problematic not only from the viewpoint of those naive idealists, but also from the viewpoint of Niebuhr's own realistic idealism, as analyzed above. Given all he had said about the human "inclination to injustice," which makes democracy necessary, how could he possibly have believed that such an imperialistic order would even remotely approximate the demands of justice? In facing this problem, he wrote:

The real question is to what degree smaller nations can be drawn into the postwar reconstruction constitutionally so that their voice and power will be fitted into the whole scheme so that it will prevent the power of the dominant elements in the organization from becoming vexatious.[145]

Niebuhr then added an amazing statement:

Fortunately, many small nations are already related to the inchoate world scheme in the United Nations. But unfortunately the policies of the United Nations are not being democratically conducted.[146]

What is amazing about this statement is that Niebuhr, the realist about human self-interest, especially collective self-interest, would think this development merely "unfortunate," as if it were simply bad luck, due to the fact that the dominant powers were not acting as morally as they might have.

The thrust of Niebuhr's whole analysis, however, implied that, given the failure of the United Nations to limit the sovereignty of the nations, the ones with the most power would use it to pursue their own perceived self-interest without considering the opinions of economically and militarily weaker nations. The same would be true of the new imperialism that Niebuhr endorsed.

"The problem of democratic justice . . . is of course a desperate problem," Niebuhr conceded.[147] But he argued against the only possibility, according to his own analysis, that would allow the problem to be even partially solved. Instead of proposing anything approaching a transnational democracy, in which all nations would participate in determining global policies, he said of "the problem of imperialism":

It includes the necessity of apportioning responsibility to the proportions of power as they actually exist. For constitutional arrangements that allowed smaller nations to determine policies, which they lacked the power to implement, could become as fruitful a source of new anarchy as unchecked dominant power could become a new source of tyranny.[148]

To see the speciousness of this argument, we could consider an analogy with US Federalism (which, Niebuhr agreed, with the World Federalists, provided the closest historical precedent for their proposal).[149] Who in the United States would argue that Montana, Utah, Nevada, New Mexico, Arizona, Vermont, Rhode Island, West Virginia, and the Dakotas should have no vote in determining policies "which they lacked the power to implement?"[150]

Niebuhr, in other words, was simply presupposing the issue at question: the continuation of global anarchy, in which each nation can press its claims only insofar as it has the economic and/or military power to back them up.

In accepting the realists' dictum that decision-making responsibility must be based on "the proportions of power as they actually exist," Niebuhr was rejecting in advance the possibility that the powerful nations, in the light of the unprecedented nature of our situation, might agree, for the sake of the survival of the human race as such, to submit themselves to a truly democratic global organization. In so doing, he was, in spite of his criticism of a completely cynical realism, accepting the dictum that human collectives never voluntarily give up power with its benefits for the sake of justice—*even if doing so is also probably necessary for the sake of their own survival.*

Niebuhr was thereby not only in effect rejecting his own view that "the human capacity for justice makes democracy possible." He was also accepting the dictum that a nation's concern for justice combined with its concern for its own long-term self-interest could never lead it to sacrifice any of its short-term advantages. In accepting this realist dictum, he sacrificed his other realist principle, according to which distributive justice can never be left to the good will of the rich and powerful. He did say, to be sure, that the organizing center of the world organization "must be surrounded by checks to prevent its power from becoming vexatious."[151] But he had, in accepting the views of the "imperialistic realists," precluded the possibility of such checks. (To take only the most obvious problem: With the United States, Britain, France, Russia, and China essentially having all the Security Council votes, who was going to place checks on the power of the North to exploit the South?)

Like the "foolish idealists" he criticized, Niebuhr opted for a too easy solution to the problem of international harmony. Like theirs, his solution, being based on the hope that the imperial powers would act with a tolerable degree of morality, was purely sentimental. He granted that the result would not be "anything like a perfect world organization."[152] But that was to understate the issue on a grand scale: Such an organization would not have even *begun* to approximate the necessary conditions, as laid out by Niebuhr's own principles, for moving toward global justice, peace, and survivability.

Given his view that nothing better than the proposal of the imperialistic realists could possibly be implemented, we can understand why Niebuhr did not undergird his theological argument for a world organization by portraying global democracy as the way to carry out the insight contained in the myth of the Messianic ruler, whose power would be matched by goodness.

In such an argument, Niebuhr could have pointed out that, although no *individual,* due to inherently limited sympathies, could even begin to approximate the divine coincidence of power and goodness, a global democracy, in which the perspectives of all nations are represented, would provide the conditions for approximating that coincidence as fully as possible within this world.

He could have added that, whereas the nations, with their individual sovereignty, serve the principle of anarchy—and thereby the demonic—a global democracy would, for the first time in history, provide a conduit for divine values to become incarnated in the international order. In this sense, the biblical dream of a reign of God on earth could be realized more fully than ever before.

In this way, Niebuhr could have marshaled not only theistic but also specifically biblical support for "the most compelling command of our day," which could have been helpful in trying to persuade America and many other nations to back this idea. But given his idea of what was realistically possible, we can understand his failure to point out that a global democracy would be the one way in which the imagined Messianic ruler's coincidence of power and goodness could be approximated in history.

Niebuhr was surely aware that he was advocating a plan falling far short of what his own analysis demanded. This awareness was suggested by his reference, just before the section entitled "Most Urgent Problem," to "the knowledge that it is not possible to build a community without the manipulation of power, and that it is not possible to use power and remain completely 'pure.'"[153]

We can refer to this contrast between *what he advocated* and *what his analysis demanded* as the gap between his political and his moral realism. His *moral* realism required that, for a global organization to have a chance of establishing peace and moving towards justice, it would have to be both powerful and democratic. By contrast, his political realism required that, for a global organization to have a chance of actually being created, it had to be far from democratic and, in fact, to be simply a continuation of the domination of the planet by the most powerful.

This gap between his moral and his political realism may partly explain why Niebuhr, after having trumpeted the cause of global government so strongly for a few years, soon subordinated it to other causes, then dropped it, and finally came to attack it.

Back in 1941, Niebuhr had argued that the cause of building a new world order, while important, "must be subordinated to the urgent, immediate task," which was "the defeat of Nazi tyranny."[154] It was in 1942–43, after that defeat seemed assured, that the task of overcoming international anarchy became the most urgent problem. In 1944, as we saw, he was still advocating a global government—even pointing out the necessity that it be democratic if justice were to be promoted—but less clearly. By 1945, although atomic weapons had been developed, the problem had become less urgent. In an essay on "The Atomic Bomb," Niebuhr pointed out that this new weapon "could make the world more secure only if a stable universal government, which would have exclusive use of the power, could be presupposed." But he then added:

> Ultimately, of course, the bomb may make for peace, because it proves that we must achieve an organized society in global terms or perish. But the prospect for the next decades, or indeed for the next century, is not reassuring.[155]

The same dispassionate analysis is reflected in his aforementioned reflections, of the same year, on the San Francisco conference to create the United Nations Organization. After pointing out that the "power-political realities" of the conference, which prevented agreement on founding an international security system, have "prompted something akin to despair among some thoughtful observers," Niebuhr added: "Such despair is premature. There may still be a possibility of gradually working out better schemes of mutual accord."[156]

Aside from the fact that the word "gradually" suggested a decline in Niebuhr's sense of urgency, he did not give any hint as to how such schemes might be gradually worked out. By 1946, the idea of world government even as a possibility for the distant future seems to have disappeared from Niebuhr's mind. In "The Conflict between Nations and Nations and between Nations and God," he argued that the latter conflict is more important.

With regard to the former, he bemoaned the fact that the victors in World War II were not using their power responsibly to promote justice but were, instead, looking out only for their own self-interest. However, rather than pointing out that this is to be expected as long as international anarchy prevails, and rather than calling on the churches to promote a world government, Niebuhr said merely that "the business of the Christian church [is] to create the spiritual atmosphere" for statesmen to give the losers the economic and political basis for a healthy existence. Rather than working to overcome nationalism, through which the nations earlier were said to serve the devil, the church was, by pointing to the fact that *all* nations are in conflict with God, to create "some decent pity and mercy to leaven the arrogance of nations."[157] This was an important task, of course; but it was a far cry from Niebuhr's earlier view, according to which the very fate of the world depended upon whether the church can convince the nations to overcome international anarchy.

Niebuhr's Rejection of World Government

By 1948, Niebuhr was no longer ignoring the issue of world government—he was attacking it. He began an editorial titled "One World or None" in this way:

> The proponents of world government, as well as many other idealists, have wearied us with the constant reiteration of the proposition that we will have no civilization at all if we do not achieve a genuine world order.[158]

Niebuhr did not remind the reader that he had been one of those wearisome "idealists" only five years earlier, or that the book that provoked the editorial, *One World or None,* was not by idealists but a number of highly regarded public figures, including Niels Bohr, Albert Einstein, Robert Oppenheimer, and fellow realist Walter Lippmann.[159] In any case, Niebuhr continued:

> The logic of this affirmation is that unless we are successful in creating a world government, powerful and good

enough to bring the lusts and ambitions of all nations under its dominion, and to substitute a vast system of mutual security for the present state of mutual fear, we will not avoid the catastrophe of mutual annihilation by atomic warfare.[160]

This statement summarized Niebuhr's own previous logic—except that he had emphasized the likelihood of this mutual annihilation even before the prospect of atomic warfare had entered the picture. Not mentioning this either, Niebuhr went on to assure the reader that although the slogan "one world or none" had a "limited justification," because it calls attention to the precarious character of our situation, it was also "a very foolish slogan."

It is foolish because any sober analysis of the contemporary scene must convince an honest student of the present impossibility of achieving world government. We do not have one world, or any hope of achieving it in the proximate future. Therefore, the logical conclusion from the slogan is that we are fated to have no world at all. Thus logic drives us to despair.[161]

Besides thereby implying that Lippmann and the other contributors were either drunk or dishonest, Niebuhr seemed also to be saying that, even if Lippmann and others with the same view were right, they should (dishonestly) keep quiet about it, so as not to drive people to despair. This would be a strange "realism."

Niebuhr's real view, however, was that Lippman and like-minded people were simply wrong, because "history is not as logical as these slogans." In a passage that suggested that his stronger doctrine of divine providence, discussed earlier, had made him more complacent, Niebuhr said:

Human society is full of all sorts of monstrous evils which, in pure logic, would destroy it. These evils persuade a devout Christian that we always live under divine judgment. But it is also true that we live by the mercy and the "long-suffering" of God. A part of this long-suffering is exhibited in the fact that the "mills of God grind slowly" and give us indeterminate chances to mend our ways and to "flee the wrath which is to come."[162]

Whereas five years earlier it had been a divine command to overcome international anarchy before it was too late, now the purpose of the appeal to God was to assure us that we have "indeterminate chances to mend our ways." By 1948, the year that he was published in *Reader's Digest, Life,* and *Time* magazine and featured on the latter's cover, Niebuhr had embraced balance-of-power realism with its consensus that world government of any type was impossible.[163]

By 1949, Niebuhr had published an article entitled "The Illusion of World Government,"[164] which (along with related writings) showed that, on this issue, there was no longer any tension between the religious and nonreligious forms of realism. Niebuhr's argument against advocates of world government contains three major points: (1) Effective governments cannot be created by fiat, (2) the nations of the world are not ready to give up national sovereignty, and (3) focusing on this utopian idea distracts attention from the immediate task at hand.

(1) The first point involves a criticism of social contract theory, with its extreme voluntarism. Against the view that governments can simply be created at will, Niebuhr argued that they presuppose the prior existence of "social tissue," consisting of "organic factors" such as ethnic kinship, a common history (usually including memory of the defeat of a common foe), a common language, a common religion and culture, and trust.[165] In other words, governments with their laws presuppose communities, and communities can only develop naturally and therefore slowly.[166] Tyrannical regimes, to be sure, can be imposed suddenly from above, but the kind of world government envisaged by its proponents, said Niebuhr, will

not be possible in the near future because the needed social tissue is far too scanty.

Writing in the early days of the Cold War, in which he had become an active participant, Niebuhr pointed to the lack of trust between the USA and the USSR as the most obvious obstacle to "one world." But the necessary tissue, he argued, was too scanty even in the noncommunist world. In this argument, he cited three factors that he had previously used to support world government, but he now used to dismiss it.

With regard to economic interdependence, he now argued that because of the wide disparities of economic strength, this factor would create extreme difficulties for allocating voting power in a world government. With respect to the fear of mutual annihilation, he said that although it does create a social force, "the fear of destruction in itself is less potent than the fear of specific peril from a particular foe. There is no record in history of peoples establishing a common community because they feared each other." And of the "inchoate sense of obligation to the inchoate community of mankind," he said: "The common moral sense is of tremendous importance for the moral and religious life of mankind; but it does not have as much immediate political relevance as is sometimes supposed."[167] Niebuhr's conclusion is that nothing better than the United Nations is now possible: A world government could emerge, if ever, only in "ages to come."[168]

(2) Niebuhr's second major point was that, even if a world government were otherwise possible, national governments are not prepared to subordinate their national sovereignty to a global democracy. The USSR, with its threat to leave the United Nations if the veto power in the Security Council were to be abolished, is only the most obvious example. America and other nations are also not ready. Besides the particular issues of the present day, there is the general historical fact: "No such explicit abnegation has ever taken place in the history of the world."[169]

(3) Niebuhr's third reason for opposing talk of world government is that it is diversionary, distracting us from the immediate, urgent task at hand: defeating Communism.

> The immediate political situation requires that we seek not only peace, but also the preservation of a civilization which we hold to be preferable to the universal tyranny with which Soviet aggression threatens us. Success in this double task is the goal; let us not be diverted from it by the pretense that there is a simple alternative.... We may have pity upon, but can have no sympathy with, those who flee to the illusory security of the impossible from the insecurities and ambiguities of the possible.[170]

This complaint, that world-government utopianism distracts us from our immediate challenges, was one that Niebuhr would repeat often in the coming decades, sometimes citing the biblical principle, "Sufficient unto the day is the evil thereof."[171]

Niebuhr's conclusion, that world government is an illusion, is one that he would hold to the end. In one of his last books, published in 1959, he put proposals for world government in the same class, in terms of naiveté, as those for unilateral disarmament.[172] In any case, aside from the issue of the validity of his arguments for this conclusion, which will be taken up later, the main question raised by the above summary of Niebuhr's thinking is how he could have been led to reverse his thinking so completely in so short a period, between 1944 and 1948.

Several factors surely played a role. Certainly very important was the one just mentioned: the propaganda effort against Communism in general and the Soviet Union in particular, in which Niebuhr played a central role. For example, his 1948 article, "For Peace, We Must Risk War," which was printed in *Reader's Digest, Time,* and *Life,* was introduced by the latter with the statement: "A distinguished theologian declares America must prevent the conquest of Germany and Western Europe by the unscrupulous Soviet tyranny."[173]

Although Niebuhr himself had run for office on the Socialist ticket some years earlier, he in 1948, in order to help Truman get reelected, helped to discredit Henry Wallace's candidacy by saying that the Communists supported it.[174] According to his biographer, he was opposed to the tactics of Joseph McCarthy, but not for the reason that most liberals were. Rather, Niebuhr thought, these tactics were bringing ridicule on the serious business of rooting out Communists.[175] He was, in this connection, in favor of the execution of the Rosenbergs as Communist spies. His 1953 piece "Why Communism is so Evil," which appeared ten days before their execution, was used ten days after it on a radio broadcast as "Ideological Special No. 256" to justify the Rosenbergs' fate. (Niebuhr would later repent of his support for their execution.)[176]

Moreover, in a *Look* essay, Niebuhr casually accused several people of being "fellow travelers," including Guy Emery Shipman, editor of the *Churchman,* which had been critical of the Soviets as far back as the 1930s. Niebuhr later admitted to Shipman that his statement was based only on impressions, as he had not had time to dig out "specific evidence." However, it was not until a year later—in 1954, after Joseph McCarthy had been discredited and the domestic Communist threat had evaporated—that Niebuhr sent a retraction to *Look.*[177]

Besides the fact that the battle with Communism would remain the "immediate" threat for the rest of Niebuhr's life, leading him to castigate "utopian" thinking as diversionary, this long-standing battle, following so closely upon the battle against the Nazi form of tyranny, seemed to solidify Niebuhr's mind into a permanently defensive mold. As we saw, he had begun as a radical reformer, seeing Christian faith as a power that could help bring about a greatly improved world. During the world wars, however, these positive efforts were put on hold in favor of single-minded concentration upon the war effort. With regard to World War II in particular, this effort meant a defense of Western civilization, warts and all, against barbarism.

Niebuhr's focus returned to positive reform of the West only after victory seemed assured. But this period was short-lived, as the conclusion of World War II virtually coincided with the rise of the Cold War, and with this rise Niebuhr's "realism" became permanently defensive, a stance for defending democracy, especially as embodied in America, as distinct from improving and extending it.

Niebuhr's extreme patriotism would not be shaken until 1966, when he said with regard to our war in Vietnam, "For the first time I fear I am ashamed of our beloved nation." Given the prior atrocities committed by this nation—including the genocide of the Native Americans, the enslavement of millions of Africans, its theft of much of Mexico, and its imperialistic adventures in Cuba and the Philippines, which led Americans such as William James and Mark Twain to form the Anti-Imperialist League—this is an amazing statement, showing how fully Niebuhr had accepted the myth of America the Good.[178]

Another factor probably contributing to Niebuhr's about-face on world government, alongside his defensive stance against Communism and his impatience with "diversionary" issues, was his increasing affiliation with Political Realists such as Hans Morgenthau and George Kennan. It would have been quite natural for Niebuhr, through occasional conversations with them and through reading their writings, to have come to share their views about world government.

These factors, however, would not provide a sufficient explanation, especially for the completeness and rapidity of Niebuhr's change of mind, unless there had been something in his theological thought that encouraged, or at least allowed, this turnabout. Had the entire thrust of his theology, as developed to that point, pointed toward global government as central to the divine purpose, Niebuhr's easy dropping of the notion would be inexplicable.

To be sure, one reason for this ease has already been intimated: the fact that the form of world government advocated by Niebuhr, one involving a hegemony exercised by the great powers, would not, by Niebuhr's own principles, have even approximated the conditions necessary to move toward a just world order. Given a cause that is wildly unpopular in one's circles and very unlikely to succeed anyway, why go to the brink on its behalf while knowing that, if it *were* to be implemented, it would not actually bring much improvement? In other words, only the idea of a truly democratic global government would have seemed worth fighting for.

But that point leads us back to the prior question: Given Niebuhr's belief that a world characterized by both peace and justice could be realized only through the creation of a global democracy, why did he not hold out for this idea? Various factors in the theological outlook with which Niebuhr began, factors that made his worldview greatly different from that of nonreligious realists, were summarized earlier. How could Niebuhr, on the basis of those theological ideas, have ended up with a *political* position so similar to that of Hans Morgenthau?

The answer is that Niebuhr did *not* do so on the basis of those early theological ideas: Niebuhr's theology had changed drastically in the period from the early 1930s, when he came to Union Theological Seminary, and 1940, when *The Nature and Destiny of Man* was taking shape. This new theology did *not* provide support for trying to clear the way for the emergence of a reign of God on earth. Accordingly, insofar as Niebuhr did have theological support for his call for world government in the early 1940s, that support was weak at best. Indeed, his later theology can be read as giving more basis for rejecting than for advocating world government. In giving up that political cause, therefore, Niebuhr was not compromising his theological principles. Indeed, he can be seen as following them more consistently.

Niebuhr's Later Theology

From the perspective of most pacifism in the usual sense, the crucial turning point in Niebuhr's thought occurred in his 1932 book, *Moral Man and Immoral Society*, because of its repudiation of nonviolence. This book was significant for our purposes, but more because of its repudiation of the Protestant quest for the Kingdom of God. As Niebuhr's biographer put it: "He dismissed with utter derision the dearest hope that animated thousands of radical liberal Christians."[179] In this book, nevertheless, Niebuhr aimed at a basic transformation of the world; indeed, it was his most aggressive book in this respect.

With regard to this issue, the crucial change began in the 1934 book, *Reflections on the End of an Era*. As mentioned earlier, this book was even more Marxian than the former one, but it also represented, theologically, a turn to the right. Being dedicated to his brother, who had recommended that he read Paul, Augustine, Luther, and Calvin, this book was his attempt to marry his own political radicalism to a theology more akin to his brother's. As he said in the preface, it combined "more conservative religious convictions and a more radical political orientation."[180] The obvious question, of course, is whether such a marriage could last. This one, at least, did not.

In any case, the "more conservative religious convictions" involved primarily sin and grace, both of which were understood more individualistically. Nevertheless, in a chapter entitled "A Radical Political Theory," Niebuhr—as a good Marxian Social Gospeler—focused on the main root of injustice, seeing it not in individual selfishness but in the accumulation of social and economic power afforded by the capitalist system.[181] In the chapter in that book entitled "The Assurance of Grace," Niebuhr spoke of the equal sin of all, saying that suffering is due to the sin that the self shares with all other selves.[182] Although this chapter still spoke of religion as providing "inspiration for morality," the accent was on a new element in Niebuhr's thought, "consolation" for "frustrations" whereby Christianity is a "supra-moral religion of grace.[183]

The religion of Jesus, said Niebuhr, provides not only ethical tension, through the demand for perfection, but also "relaxation," to "reduce the strain of living in an imperfect world."[184] Another word for relaxation is "serenity," which comes through realizing that one's imperfections are understood and sympathetically appreciated.[185] The twofold need, Niebuhr said, is to "accommodate the vision of perfection to an imperfect world" while still "retaining the urge to perfect the world."[186] It is not easy, Niebuhr observed, to preserve a "decent balance" between these two sides: The religious need for reconciliation is likely to lead one to accept a "premature peace." From a perspective critical of Niebuhr's later balance between these two aspects of Christian faith, these lines seem prophetic.

In Niebuhr's late theology, the balance shifted from moral striving to "religious peace," from the "strenuous mood" to "assurance" and "relaxation," and from the Kingdom of God in history to the fulfillment of life "beyond history." Indeed, Niebuhr's biographer reported that, in 1937, Niebuhr was brought to Oxford in advance of the next meeting of the World Assembly in order to "help bury any lingering Kingdom talk" that had been generated by the Assembly in Stockholm.[187] This shift, from "the urge to perfect the world" to an accommodation to this world's imperfection on the basis of a transcendent fulfillment, involved every aspect of Niebuhr's theology.

With regard to the doctrine of God, Niebuhr shared, as we saw, Whitehead's view that God is doubly related to the world: God influences the world by providing ideals for actualization, and then the world is taken up into what Whitehead called God's "consequent nature." This second aspect, which involves God's omniscient, sympathetic reception of the world into the divine "everlastingness" (Whitehead) or "eternity" (Niebuhr), can be characterized as both judgment and forgiveness. In Niebuhr's later thought, this second side of God's relation to the world became dominant over the first.

Using the language of "grace," Niebuhr contrasted "grace as power" with "grace as pardon." The former is "an actual 'power of righteousness,'" which heals the contradiction within our hearts"; the latter is grace "conceived as 'justification,' as pardon rather than power, as the forgiveness of God."[188] Niebuhr, following St. Paul, held the latter to be primary.[189]

Niebuhr's view of the two sides of the gospel cohered with his doctrine of divine power in relation to history:

> The problem of history . . . is not that God should be revealed as strong enough to overcome the defiance of the evil against His will; but as having resources of mercy great enough to redeem as well as to judge all men.[190]

That statement came directly after Niebuhr's statement that "the consummation of history cannot be a Messianic reign . . . which resolves the conflicts of history in a reign of peace."[191] Niebuhr's doctrine of divine power in history, accordingly, was not such as to dispose him to expect a solution to the problem of war.

Consistent with the subordination of "grace in us" to "grace over us" is the fact that Niebuhr's theology contains no "christology proper," no discussion of the distinctive presence of God in Jesus. As mentioned in the first section of this chapter, Niebuhr (rightly) rejected the traditional christological discussions as metaphysical nonsense. Unlike many liberal theologians, however, he made no attempt to replace such nonsense with a way to express in metaphysical terms how God could have been present in Jesus.

What this amounted to is that Niebuhr's christology contained no account of divine grace as a power *in* Jesus, and thereby no account of Jesus as especially incarnating divine ideals for the world. Rather, in line with the priority of grace *over* us, Niebuhr said that "the Atonement is the significant content of the Incarnation."[192] By

"Atonement" Niebuhr did not, of course, mean some supernatural transaction. He meant revelation—revelation of "the mercy and the justice of God in their paradoxical relationship"[193]—by virtue of which the divine mercy forgives our failure to live up to the law of love: "The revelation of the Atonement . . . discloses a transcendent divine mercy which represents . . . God's freedom over His own law."[194] It is, accordingly, Jesus on the cross, not also Jesus proclaiming the Kingdom of God, who is revelatory:

> To declare, as Jesus does, that the Messiah, the representative of God, must suffer, is to make vicarious suffering the final revelation of meaning in history. But it is the vicarious suffering of the representative of God, and not of some force in history, which finally clarifies the obscurities of history and discloses the sovereignty of God over history.[195]

Niebuhr then added:

> It is God Who suffers for man's iniquity. He takes the sins of the world upon and into Himself. This is to say that the contradictions of history are not resolved in history; but they are only ultimately resolved on the level of the eternal and the divine.[196]

All of these aspects of Niebuhr's christology fit with his rejection of the idea that Jesus somehow provided a solution to the problem of history.

> The Messianic Age did not fulfill the ideal potentialities of human nature and history but offered instead a 'reconciliation' between God and man. . . . Thus the story of the life of Jesus with the death on the cross became, for Christianity, the initial statement of a "realistic" interpretation of human history.[197]

Accordingly, Niebuhr's christology, part of the very meaning of which is that "the contradictions of history are not resolved in history," would not have predisposed him to expect any clue within it—such as the idea of a Messianic ruler combining power and goodness—for overcoming the problems of war and injustice.

The same is true for his doctrine of history as such. The main target of Niebuhr's discussion about history was the optimistic view according to which progress—moral as well as technological—is inevitable, somehow built into the nature of things. In opposition to this view, Niebuhr offered a more tragic view of history, based on the realization that "every heightened potency of human existence may also represent a possibility of evil."[198]

In other words, "history cannot move forward towards increasing cosmos without developing possibilities of chaos by the very potencies which have enhanced cosmos."[199] Niebuhr was absolutely right on this point. But he tended to turn the "possibilities" into necessities, so that increases in good are *necessarily* accompanied by increases in evil (not simply increased *possibilities* for evil). The optimistic view of history arising in the Renaissance, said Niebuhr, "did not recognize that every new human potency may be an instrument of chaos as well as of order."[200] But Niebuhr tended to treat the "may be" as an inevitability. By blurring this distinction, Niebuhr assumed that good and evil will necessarily continue to grow in tandem.

Saying that "Jesus anticipates the growth of evil as well as the growth of good in history," Niebuhr pointed to the symbol of the antichrist, saying that it should be taken seriously (albeit not literally) to refute the equation of historical progress with the kingdom of God: "The Antichrist stands at the end of history to indicate that history cumulates, rather than solves, the essential problems of human existence."[201] We cannot, accordingly, look forward to a time, whether measured in decades, centuries, or millennia, in which God will reign on earth: "History is not its own redeemer. The 'long run' of it is no more redemptive in the ultimate sense than the 'short run.'"[202]

One might think that Niebuhr was here speaking only of our trying to redeem history on our own, without the assistance of divine grace. But in endorsing the Reformation doctrine of "justification by faith," he said that it "represents the final renunciation in the heart of Christianity of the human effort to complete life and history, *whether with or without divine grace.*"[203]

In any case, with regard to our issue in particular, Niebuhr said: "The political life of man must constantly steer between the Scylla of anarchy and the Charybdis of tyranny."[204] Even world government, he implied, would not enable us finally to transcend this alternative:

> The actual historic achievements of man in history, his creation of larger and larger units of "brotherhood,"...are always corrupted by the twin evils of the tyrannical subordination of life to life and the anarchic conflict of life with life. There is therefore no...hope of history gradually purifying itself.[205]

Niebuhr here seemed to say that a worldwide community, which would overcome anarchy, would necessarily result in a global tyranny. Accordingly, Christian faith for Niebuhr did not provide a basis for hope that evil will finally be defeated in history.

Rather than his (non-Manichean) faith leading him to assume that there *must* be some way to get beyond the hitherto perennial problems of history, his last version of Christian faith assured him that history "has no solution of its own problem."[206] Therefore, for Niebuhr to have held up the idea of democratic global government in the early 1940s, portraying it as a demythologized version of the ideal ruler in whom goodness and power are combined and by means of which we could get beyond the problems of anarchy, tyranny, and injustice, would have been to contradict the theological-ethical-political position he had been constructing during the previous decade.

We began this review of Niebuhr's later theology with his doctrine of God, in particular his twofold doctrine of divine grace. Now, having looked at his christology, his doctrine of salvation, and his view of history, we need to return to his doctrine of God, this time looking at his assumptions as to the meaning of history and the nature of sin from the divine standpoint.

Part of Niebuhr's account would lead us to believe that the ultimate good is harmony with God and fellow creatures, so that the basic sin would involve lack of harmony in this sense. For example, in explicating Jesus' statement about the greatest commandment, Niebuhr said: "What is commanded is . . . a harmony between the soul and God . . . a harmony within the soul . . . and a harmony between the self and the neighbour."[207] And, speaking of "man" (using the language of the time), Niebuhr said: "He knows that he ought to act so as to assume only his rightful place in the harmony of the whole."[208] Niebuhr sometimes described sin in line with this view of the ultimate norm:

> Sin is occasioned precisely by the fact that man refuses to admit his "creatureliness" and to acknowledge himself as merely a member of a total unity of life. . . . The law of his nature is love, a harmonious relation of life to life in obedience to the divine centre and source of his life. This law is violated when man seeks to make himself the centre. . . . Man, in other words, is a sinner not because he is one limited individual within a whole but rather because he is betrayed by his very ability to survey the whole to imagine himself the whole.[209]

From this perspective, one would assume that, from the divine perspective, the primary problem with human beings is their violation of the harmony of the whole, so that God's primary concern in our time would be that human beings find a way to live in harmony with each other and the rest of the planet's life. Assuming that a democratic global government would be a necessary condition for such a harmony to be realized, our creating such a government should be at the top of the divine list of priorities for the human race. God would be trying to get us to realize that the imperative to overcome global anarchy is, as Niebuhr at one time put it, "the most compelling command of our day."

However, far more passages in Niebuhr's writings show that this idea of harmony, in which each member's self-interest is adjusted so that it is compatible with the good of the whole, was not good enough. That ideal, which is called "mutual love," is generally said to be inferior to "self-sacrificial love," the true Christian norm, according to which overcoming sin requires an even more stringent ideal: "What is demanded is an action in which regard for the self is completely eliminated."[210] Any self-interest whatsoever, even if it be in harmony with the interests of all others, is sinful: "The final goodness...stands in contradiction to all forms of human goodness in which self-assertion and love are compounded."[211] One may protest, of course, that such an ideal is impossible; but that was precisely Niebuhr's point:

> Christ as the norm of human nature defines the final perfection of man in history. This perfection . . . is the perfection of sacrificial love. The same Cross which symbolizes the love of God . . . also indicates that the perfection of man is not attainable in history.[212]

It is this (impossible) ideal of human perfection that stands behind Niebuhr's "paradoxical" assertion, examined in this chapter's first section, that sin is not necessary but inevitable. Although Niebuhr sought to deny it, he in effect made sin a necessary consequence of finitude, at least finitude equipped with power to survey the whole, see itself as one among many, and understand the divine norm.

Nevertheless, by portraying the failure to eliminate all self-interest as a misuse of freedom, for which we are responsible, Niebuhr called it "sin." One could complain, of course, that to believe that we sin inevitably would drive us to despair. But that, too, was precisely Niebuhr's aim: He had come to accept Reformation theology's view that the highest good of which we are capable is to realize that we are not capable of any good and to throw ourselves upon the divine mercy to forgive our sin. If that is the highest good, then the worst sin is the proud refusal to admit our own insufficiency:

> Without . . . despair there is no possibility of the contribution which appropriates the divine forgiveness. It is in this contrition and in this appropriation of divine mercy and forgiveness that the human situation is fully understood and overcome. In this experience man understands himself in his finiteness, realizes the guilt of his efforts to escape his insufficiency and dependence and lays hold upon a power beyond himself which both completes his incompleteness and purges him of his false and vain efforts at self-completion.[213]

It is really *this* issue, Niebuhr in effect said, that is really important to God. Whether we are properly contrite about the sinfulness that remains even in our best actions is more important than the distinction between better and worse actions. Although the distinction between the righteous and the evildoers is important, it pales in significance before the fact that "the righteous are not righteous before the divine judgment."[214]

Whereas the earlier definition of sin suggested that the ultimate problem of history faced by God would be how to overcome our disharmony with ourselves, other creatures, and the will of God for the good of the whole, this second conception of sin suggests a different account: "The real problem of history is the proud pretension of all human endeavors, which seeks to obscure their finite and partial character."[215]

From this perspective, the chief problem raised for Christian faith by history is not that, although it is said to be providentially guided by a good Creator, evil seems to be triumphing over good: The issue of "the ambiguity of the momentary triumph of evil yields to the question of how God will complete history by overcoming the perennial evil in every human good."[216] The final question is "not how the righteous will gain victory over the unrighteous, but how the evil in every good and the unrighteousness of the righteous is to be overcome."[217] God, in short, seemed to be less concerned about the good of the whole than about our individual dispositions.

This dimension of Niebuhr's thought, which really became its central theme, was supported by another feature of his idea of God, which was discussed earlier: his traditional idea that God is "eternal" and thereby knows the whole of history—past, present, and future—simultaneously. This doctrine, for one thing, suggested that the future of the planet is *not* now undecided but somehow eternally known by God. This thought could make the creation of a world order to overcome war and injustice seem less urgent.

This doctrine also suggested, Niebuhr's insistence to the contrary notwithstanding, that history is not ultimately meaningful from the divine perspective, because the temporal process really contributes nothing to God. With regard to the issue at hand, this means that God has no "interest" in the world—that is, that the divine self is not realizing any kind of self-fulfillment through the world. Relevant in this regard is Niebuhr's endorsement of Anders Nygren's contention that Christian *agape* is to be completely devoid of self-interest.[218]

For Nygren, this claim was based on the idea that our love is to imitate the divine *agape,* which is completely outgoing, self-giving, disinterested love, because God has nothing to gain from the world. Niebuhr, in sanctioning *agape,* understood as sacrificial love, and by appealing to "the character of God" as the norm,[219] would seem to be presupposing the same idea of God.

This set of ideas about God, sin, and history is strongly in tension with the view that overcoming anarchy would be of utmost concern from the divine perspective. Viewing the world from "the standpoint of the eternal" would undermine, rather than undergird, the importance of this issue. As Niebuhr became preoccupied with the Soviet Union and Communism, so that the emergence of any kind of global government came to seem more unlikely and concern with it diversionary, he could have easily decided that overcoming anarchy, which he already had put in a secondary spot on the divine list of priorities, was not really on the list at all.

Indeed, some of Niebuhr's statements could be interpreted to mean that the effort to achieve a global government would be a manifestation of our basic sin. In any case, this view by Niebuhr would have reinforced the conclusion, already implied by his christology, eschatology, and doctrine of grace, that overcoming global anarchy is not mandated by Christian faith in our time.

Niebuhr's Realism and the Nuclear Dilemma

The upshot of the above discussion is that, although Niebuhr began with a theological position that could have led to a religious realism significantly different in its political implications from Political Realism as usually understood, his later theology supported a political position devoid of much difference, as illustrated by his approach to Communism. His failure to advocate a truly democratic form of global governance, followed by his eventual acceptance of conventional balance-of-power realism, accordingly, was simply part of a more general failure. Late in life, Niebuhr himself in effect admitted the bankruptcy of this kind of realism in the nuclear age.

At one time, he had been somewhat complacent about the danger posed by nuclear weapons. In the 1950s, Niebuhr considered the H-bomb perilous—not, however, primarily because of its destructiveness, but because it might tempt us either to a quick-fix or to "sentimental idealism."[220] His biographer reported, for example, Niebuhr was dismayed to discover that the students at Columbia University were so morally disturbed by the prospect of nuclear war that they were considering pacifism.[221] Niebuhr's view in those days was that we must "dismiss" fears of nuclear war in order to summon the fortitude to protect the "soft spots" in the world from Communism for decades; we should not even rule out a first use of nuclear weapons. As late as 1959 he said that, "to serve peace, we must threaten war without blinking the fact that the threat may be a factor in precipitating war."[222] We must run this risk, he said, even though such a war could mean the total annihilation of the civilization we were seeking to defend.[223]

By this time, however, Niebuhr was no longer complacent. In an essay entitled "Reinhold Niebuhr's Social Ethic," John Bennett said of Niebuhr that nuclear weapons created for him "an almost intolerable dilemma."[224] That dilemma, in Niebuhr's words in 1959, was that the West "cannot guard its treasures, accumulated through the ages, against a new despotism without running the risk of a suicidal war."[225] The dilemma was put in moral terms in 1958, when he wondered

> why our leaders were so complacent about the fact that physical survival seemed now to mean our moral annihilation.... For even without the hydrogen bomb, a dozen Nagasaki bombs in Europe and Asia would mean the destruction of any moral claims for our civilization.[226]

We could, in other words, preserve the values of our civilization through the use of these weapons only by showing that we have no values worth preserving. The dilemma is that, with global anarchy armed with weapons of mass destruction, the only options for political leaders—either fail to defend one's people and its way of life or risk physical annihilation—are both morally abhorrent. Although by 1959 Niebuhr had greatly relativized his early moral contrast between the American and Soviet empires and spoke of the need to think in terms of co-existence,[227] he still maintained that we had to continue threatening to use nuclear weapons, which meant that there could be no "moral answer to the nuclear dilemma."[228]

In 1961, reflecting on the possibility that we would be attacked with nuclear weapons and would respond in kind, Niebuhr asked rhetorically: "Could a civilization loaded with the monstrous guilt (connected with a nuclear catastrophe) have enough moral health to survive?"[229] Niebuhr reportedly remarked more than once that, if a nuclear attack came, he wanted to be among the first to be killed, because he would not want to be involved in deciding what to do.

The dead end to which his kind of realism helped lead Niebuhr could not have been more poignantly expressed. Had he foreseen this dead end in the early 1940s, might he have held out for the ideal of a global democratic government, as quixotic as it may have seemed, as the only possible moral answer to the dilemmas of modern political life? Or, having seen that a full-fledged global government, conceived as the US Federal Government writ large, is neither possible nor desirable, might he, by continuing to reflect upon the issue, have realized that his two central concerns—overcoming war and moving toward economic justice—require a much less extensive global agency, which *could* be advocated as really possible?

Summary

Such an eventuality would have been more likely had Niebuhr had a theology to support it. As it was, however, he did not. His understanding of Jesus's ethic was not directly relevant to politics at all. His christology more generally, in conjunction with his doctrine of God, was intended not to inspire us to solve the global political problems of peace and justice but to console us for our inevitable failure to do so. His doctrine of sin, by subordinating the problem of harmony to that of pride—the social problem to the issue of individual disposition—reduced the issue of international peace and justice to secondary status at best. Niebuhr's doctrine of God as eternal, enjoying a simultaneous perception of past, present, and future, threatened even this secondary status by implicitly undermining Niebuhr's claim that the historical process was ultimately meaningful.

This idea of God, especially in conjunction with the notion that the most serious human problem is pride, not disharmony, would discourage the idea that the theologian's task, by virtue of trying to see the world from the divine perspective, entails focusing on the long-term sustainability of the planet. The idea that history is meaningful was further undermined by Niebuhr's tragic view of history, according to which every increase in good will always be matched by a corresponding increase in evil. (He should have said: "every increase in *the possibility* of good will always be matched by a corresponding increase in *the possibility* of evil.")

Niebuhr's ambiguous position on divine power further weakened the basis provided by his theology for political effort: On the one hand, Niebuhr's movement toward divine omnipotence, according to which at least the large-scale events of history are determined by "a mysterious divine sovereignty," would, if taken seriously, lead toward complacency and quietism. On the other hand, Niebuhr's notion that God—at least God as seeking to incarnate ideals in the world—is permanently defeated in history provides no basis for hope that things can ever be made significantly better.

In fact, this idea, that our awareness of ideals involves God's influence upon our experience, is the only part of Niebuhr's later theology that provides a distinctively religious impetus for moral-political effort. And yet Niebuhr ended up agreeing with other realists that ideals are largely impotent, especially with regard to international relations. Niebuhr's theology, in short, provided no basis for hope for our world. In his later period, he suggested, wishfully, that despair can be creative.[230]

Reinhold Niebuhr was arguably wiser in his earlier, radical period, when he said that great moral effort usually requires the conviction that, because history is ultimately behind one's cause, success is likely.

6

Against the Threefold Veto of Global Democracy

A S NOTED IN CHAPTER 2, the idea a of a global government has
been discussed since the eighteenth century. However, besides
the obvious fact that it has not been created, many thinkers have
explicitly argued against the idea. Some of them have offered
a threefold argument: that global government would be (1)
unnecessary, (2) that it would not be desirable, and that it would,
in any case, be (3) impossible. I will argue that, although some of
these arguments had merit in the past, they are no longer valid,
because the world has changed fundamentally. I will argue that
global democratic government is now *necessary* for the survival of
civilization, that its creation would be highly *desirable* for many
other reasons as well, and that there are even reasons to consider
it *possible*.

Before beginning this threefold argument, however, I should
briefly indicate what I do and do not mean by a global government.
I mean a *federation*, in which the various countries could maintain
their integrity and most of their present powers. This federation

would be based on the principle of *subsidiarity,* according to which authority to deal with some particular issue would be exercised at the lowest, most local, level at which it can be done effectively. The global level of government would be allocated authority to deal only with those issues that can be effectively addressed only at the global level. Besides preventing war, these issues would include climate destruction, global pandemics, human rights, and the global economy.

Moreover, this government would embody democracy. It is widely held that it is good for nations to be democratic. Insofar as this idea is accepted, it would seem to follow that it would be ideal that civilization as a whole would be democratic.

A global government of this type would not fit the image that is often conjured up by talk of a "world state," or "world government," in which all power is concentrated at the top. This global federation would not, furthermore, be imposed by one part of the world on the rest. Rather, it would be based on a global democratic constitution, complete with a *global bill of rights and responsibilities* that would be worked out by representatives from all peoples, then ratified by these peoples themselves. For this reason, this book's title speaks not simply of global government in general, but of "global democracy" in particular.

It would have a *legislature,* through which the representatives of the world's people could finally become self-legislating, and an *executive branch* to enforce these laws.[1] There would be a world *judiciary system* with mandatory jurisdiction, through which the constitution would be interpreted and applied and through which disputes between countries would be settled peacefully—rather than, as now, through war or its threat. There would also be a *global police* force to enforce the orders from the executive and judicial branches.

But there would be no global military force. This would be unneeded because the nations will have disarmed, because war would no longer be necessary; it would even be unthinkable—just as war is unthinkable between California and Colorado, in spite of their water disputes. So likewise the global government would need only a police force designed to enforce the laws enacted by the global legislature and judiciary. With this brief sketch, I turn to the question of why the creation of such a government is now necessary, otherwise desirable, and possible.

Why Global Democracy is Necessary

In arguing that global democracy is now *necessary*, I am using the term in the strictest sense: necessary for the very survival of human civilization.Political leaders have always given highest priority to what they have called "reasons of state," meaning those things necessary for the very survival of the state. Such things have always been taken to trump all other considerations. Although thus far most of our political leaders have not realized it, at least publicly, reasons of human survival must now trump what have traditionally been considered reasons of state. This fact was stated early in the twentieth century, most famously in Goldsworthy Lowes Dickinson's 1926 book, *The International Anarchy*, in which he had said (as pointed out in Chapter 4): "Whenever and wherever the anarchy of armed States exists, war [becomes] inevitable."[2]

War and Nuclear Weapons

All discussions of the need for a global government, from the eighteenth century forward, have said that global government is necessary to overcome the war-system. In the twentieth century, this argument took on new urgency, because overcoming the war-system came to be seen as necessary for survival. For example, prior to Lowes Dickinson's 1926 book, he had written in 1917 that, without a global institution that can prevent war, civilization is doomed. For modern war, equipped by modern science, is incompatible with the continuance of an industrial civilisation. A change has taken place in the last century which cuts us off absolutely from all the preceding history of mankind. We have learned how to use or misuse nature, and we hold in our hands the powers of life and death.[3]

It was after the creation of atomic weapons, however, that this argument became widely stated. For example, the eminent historian William McNeill, whose 1980 study *The Pursuit of Power* traced the development of the technology of warfare over the past 1000 years, concluded his study by saying:

> To halt the arms race,... nothing less radical than [a global sovereign power] seems in the least likely to suffice.... The alternative appears to be the sudden and total annihilation of the human species.[4]

In a 1982 book entitled *Confronting War,* Ronald Glossop wrote: "The war problem has become the most urgent problem facing the human race. Either the war problem gets solved or humanity risks extinction."[5] He added that the world has been much too optimistic about the continued nonuse of nuclear weapons, because:

> Optimism about nonuse of nuclear weapons by major powers overlooks the logic of war and the tremendous advantage which comes from using nuclear weapons first rather than second. The aim of war is to use military power to win, to impose one's will on the other side. In such a situation if either side were facing defeat, it would use nuclear weapons rather than surrender. At the same time the side which was winning the war would want to use its nuclear weapons before sustaining such an attack from a desperate opponent.[6]

At the front of his book, Glossup quoted a 1983 statement by Sydney Lens, which said:

> World government is an idea whose time has come. ... In the past it was simply considered desirable by certain philosophers. ... Now, however, it has become indispensable to the survival of civilization.[7]

The most famous person who came to work passionately for global government because of the development of nuclear weapons was Albert Einstein, who had been partly responsible for this development. Einstein called world government "the most important goal of our time."[8] In making his famous statement that the atomic bomb has changed everything except our way of thinking, Einstein had in mind our thinking about world order. "As long as the present condition of international anarchy prevails," he said, "all of us will continue to live under the constant threat of sudden annihilation."[9] Einstein felt so strongly about this issue that he refused to lend his name to halfway measures. For example, having been asked to sign the resolutions of a peace conference in which Thomas Mann had participated, Einstein declined, saying:

> The resolutions are not far-reaching enough to solve the problem of international security. That goal can be attained only by creating a world government with authority to settle conflicts on the basis of law. ... No less radical a measure will call a halt to the arms race and prevent war.[10]

In response to a fellow pacifist who thought it was inconsistent of Einstein to support the war against Nazi Germany while calling himself a pacifist, Einstein replied:

> I am indeed a pacifist, but ... I am of the conviction that realization of the goal of pacifism is possible only through supranational organization. To stand unconditionally for this cause is, in my opinion, the criterion of true pacifism.[11]

I quote this last statement by Einstein partly because I myself struggled in the 1980s with the issue of how one could be a pacifist in a nuclear world. Trying to work out what I was calling a "post-nuclear theology," I could find no satisfactory position. On the one hand, I agreed with Reinhold Niebuhr and other Political Realists that traditional pacifism is not a morally responsible option in our present world. On the other hand, I agreed with the pacifists that the defense of nuclear deterrence by Niebuhr and other Christian Realists was both contrary to the Christian gospel and ultimately self-defeating because eventually bound to fail.[12] It was only in the early 1990s, primarily through the influence of Einstein, McNeill's *Pursuit of Power,* Andrew Schmookler's *Parable of the Tribes,* and a lecture by Richard Falk on global anarchy[13] that I found a way to combine Christian pacifism with political realism.[14]

In any case, Ronald Glossup's warning not to be optimistic about the continued nonuse of nuclear weapons should still be heeded, in spite of the end of the Cold War. Indeed, Helen Caldicott, in her 2002 book *The New Nuclear Danger,* argued that the threat of nuclear holocaust by then was greater than ever.[15] In particular, we know that there are many nuclear weapons and many nuclear materials that have not been well-protected, that there are terrorist groups who are probably trying to obtain nuclear weapons, and that some of them would probably like to use them for revenge. It is also the case that the use of nuclear weapons against American troops or civilians might well lead the United States to launch nuclear missiles toward Russia and/or China, which might well then respond in kind. It has long been known, furthermore, that even a relatively small exchange of nuclear weapons might initiate a "nuclear winter," in which little life could survive. The sudden extinction of human civilization, about which we have been repeatedly warned, could occur at any time.

One particularly chilling incident reported by Caldicott occurred in 1995, when Russian military personnel concluded that an American missile launched off the coast of Norway was the beginning of a nuclear war. The Russian computer containing nuclear launch codes was opened in front of then-President Boris Yeltsin, who had only three minutes in which to decide whether to launch missiles toward the USA (at a time at which he may have been inebriated). Luckily, the US missile changed course at the last minute. But if Yeltsin had launched Russia's missiles, they would have been detected by America's early-warning satellites and President Clinton (who may well have been preoccupied) would have then had three minutes to make his decision.[16]

The Burning of Fossil Fuels

Even if civilization somehow manages to continue surviving its game of Russian roulette with nuclear weapons, however, another threat to extinction lies in waiting. Unless civilization drastically changes its present trajectory of burning fosseil fuels, which is warming the atmosphere and the ocean, human extinction will follow.

The global environmental crisis, like the problems of war, imperialism, and terrorism, can be solved only by a global democratic government. The problem with the present system, with its anarchical order of sovereign states, was brought out by President George Bush the elder after the Earth Summit in 1992. Asked why he refused to sign the biodiversity treaty, Bush declared: "I am President of the United States, not president of the world and I'll do what is best to defend US interests."[17] The problem is highlighted by the title of an article in which this statement is quoted: "Earth at the Mercy of National Interests." Until these partial, competitive, shortsighted national interests are trumped by a government whose leaders are mandated to represent the long-term common good, our planet will be headed toward ecocide.[18] For us passively to allow this trajectory to continue would be the height of irresponsibility. Global democracy is necessary if human civilization is not to be destroyed by the excessive use of fossil fuels

The environmental problem and the problems of militarism and imperialism are, furthermore, closely connected. For one thing, the planet's armed forces are probably its single largest polluter, using 7% of the world's oil and causing perhaps 30% of the total environmental destruction. A jet fighter, for example, uses as much fuel in an hour as a US motorist in a whole year, and a B-52 bomber uses 14 times that much.[19]

A second connection is the fact that militarism, commanding the largest segment of the world's governmental spending each year, wastes the tax monies that could be used to overcome poverty and environmental problems. For example, the report issued from the Earth Summit in 1992 said that the planet's most serious environmental crises could be overcome if its peoples would spend $600 billion a year for 10 years. But the governments of the world, saying they could not afford this much, pledged only a measly total of $5 billion. Every year, however, the governments of the world spend $1 *trillion*—that's $1,000 billion—for military purposes, with the United States spending more than the next eight or so countries combined. If we would put an end to the war system, we would not only stop the most polluting and resource-depleting enterprise on earth but also have hundreds of billions of dollars to address environmental problems. Alternative technologies that could prevent runaway climate change are already available. All that is needed is the will to apply them. But that will has not existed. This is even more the case since the presidency of George W. Bush, who, as Thomas Friedman put it, "made 'conservation' a dirty word," and which was made even dirtier by the Trump administration.[20]

The attitude of the Bush Administration pointed to a third connection between militarism and the global environmental crisis: As long as the war-system exists, the immediate military threats to a country's security will always seem more urgent to its political leaders than the longer-term threats posed by environmental deterioration, so that the warnings of environmentalists will seem an annoying distraction. From a longer-term perspective, however, the overarching question of the present century is whether human civilization will find a sustainable way to live on this planet before we destroy its capacity to sustain life. It is war that is the distraction. At the very time when the two major threats to human civilization are 1) fighting wars and 2) burning oil and natural gas, our leaders are devoted to planning wars *for* oil and gas.

Why Global Democracy is Desirable

Besides the fact that global democratic government is necessary if we are to have a realistic hope that civilization will not be soon destroyed, there are also many other reasons why it is desirable.

In the past, most discussions of global government have argued that a global government would be *un*desirable. For example, in an important book in 1959 titled *Man, the State, and War*, Neo-Realist Kenneth Waltz warned of the possibility that "a world state would be a world tyranny" in which "we might find ourselves . . . living a life worse than death."[21]

But this argument was answered long ago by Thomas Hobbes, who said that although people tend to fear the possible consequences of a single supreme power,

> yet the consequences of the want of it, which is perpetual war . . . are much worse. The condition of man in this life shall never be without inconveniences.[22]

As David Gauthier said in his important study of Hobbes's political theory:

> Hobbes states a fundamentally important principle in this argument. . . . The alternative to an intolerable situation is never an ideal situation, but rather a barely tolerable situation. We must replace presently intolerable risks by tolerable ones.[23]

Hobbes, to be sure, was talking about the need for a supreme power in a localized region. He even specifically argued against the need for a global government. His argument was that, as Kenneth Waltz put it, although anarchy breeds war, it "so far has not made life itself impossible." This is why, Waltz said, that the logic that shows world government to be the solution to war "does not carry men . . . to the founding of a world state."[24] But that was 300 years ago. In the meantime, as Gauthier argued, the creation of nuclear weapons has so changed the situation that international anarchy is as threatening to our security as local anarchy would be, so that today Hobbes would consider world government necessary.[25] Einstein made a similar point, saying:

> I agree . . . with respect to the dangers which would be involved in the creation of a world government. But I believe that these dangers are less significant than the dangers of the international anarchy which, in fact, involves the perpetual threat of war. It seems to me that the latter is the most effective means by which government can keep the people in some sort of slavery.[26]

The truth of Einstein's final point seems to be verified by the fact that the so-called war on terror has been used to justify a draconian scaling back of human rights.[27]

The danger that a global government might become tyrannical should not, of course, be ignored. It should be taken extremely seriously as representatives of the various nations come together to work out a constitution for a global government. All that we know about the way checks and balances can prevent any one branch of government from acquiring absolute power must be built in. There should be a Bill of Rights and Responsibilities not only for individuals but also for member nations in the global federation.[28]

Two concerns should be addressed with the utmost care. One of these would be the global police force. As pointed out earlier, there would be no military, war-fighting establishment at the global level, because the nations would not have armies. But the global police force would need a preponderance of power. It could, thereby, become dangerous. Those designing it would need to reduce the danger to the absolute minimum by various measures, such as ensuring that leadership positions were always distributed among officers from all parts of the world. Although some danger would still remain, the danger is nothing compared with the present situation, in which the US government is well on the way to seeing itself as having sufficient military power to defeat the militaries of the rest of the world combined. We must not, as Hobbes and Gautier have emphasized, let a small, possible danger frighten us from instituting the one form of world order that could overcome the enormous danger that is already a present reality.

Plutocracy

The other danger is that the global government would become a plutocracy, captured by the wealthiest individuals and corporations of the world to serve their narrow interests. That might seem a danger impossible to prevent, since the framers of the US Constitution, as wise as they were, failed to prevent this from happening in America. They did not, however, fail in spite of trying. They did not try, as they themselves were plutocrats, who believed that the wealthy *should* rule.[29]

Those who are *genuine democrats*, believing that the people of the world should rule themselves, could rather easily devise means to keep money out of global politics, starting with the public financing of all elections—which is, incidentally, the first step that the people of America need to take to replace our plutocracy with a democracy. The difference between the two systems is that a democracy works by the principle of "one person, one vote," whereas plutocracy's operating principle is "one dollar, one vote." In a plutocracy, a single corporation with billions of dollars can outvote millions of people.

The alarm about corporate plutocracy was sounded already by Abraham Lincoln. Reflecting the fact that corporations had grown tremendously in size and influence during the Civil War, Lincoln said, shortly before his assassination:

> Corporations have been enthroned. . . . The money power will endeavor to prolong its reign by working on the prejudices of the people . . . until wealth is aggregated in a few hands . . . and the Republic is destroyed.[30]

Lincoln had famously defined democracy as government of the people, by the people, and for the people. A subsequent president, Rutherford Hayes, said that democracy had been replaced by "a government of corporations, by corporations, and for corporations."[31] Perhaps the crucial event was in 1886. Having succeeded in obtaining a pro-business Supreme Court, the corporations got the Court to reverse previous rulings by declaring corporations "legal persons," which gave them all the protections of the US Bill of Rights, including free speech.[32] This ruling, by allowing corporations, with their billions of dollars, into the political process, completely subverted the democratic principle of political equality and achieved, in the words of businessman Paul Hawken, "precisely what the Bill of Rights was intended to prevent: domination of public thought and discourse."[33] This is the most serious failing of the current American system, which a constitution for democracy at the global level would need to prevent. This failing became even worse when the US Supreme Court allowed the passage (in 2010) of the terribly named *Citizens United.*

A global democratic government, whatever its shortcomings turn out to be in regulating global finance, will still be a great improvement over the present system of global governance, which is *fully* plutocratic. This is the case whether one regards global governance as exercised by the G7 nations, which are among the richest in the world, or simply by the United States. The policies of all these countries are, furthermore, controlled by the richest five or even one percent of their populations. So global governance is now carried out in terms of policies that serve the interests of an extremely tiny, but extremely wealthy, minority. The likelihood that any global democratic government that is instituted will be far from perfect should not, again, deter us from the one solution that could put an end to the extreme plutocracy that is the present reality.

Human Rights

One of the major moral problems of the present world order is that, although the acceptance by the United Nations of the Universal Declaration of Human Rights has enshrined human rights in international law, these rights are as widely violated now as they were earlier. The extent to which people are still unprotected, unless they happen to live in a state that guarantees human rights, was shown by the massacre in Rwanda in 1994. Although it was widely known in advance that the massacre of the Tutsis by the Hutus was going to occur, a million unarmed people, including 300,000 children, were slaughtered over a period of three months, while the world's leaders, knowing full well what was going on, did nothing. This was no spontaneous outbreak of "ethnic violence," but a systematic slaughter, based on lists of names and carried out in broad daylight. Each group of killers had been "trained to kill 1,000 human beings every twenty minutes," and garbage trucks had been organized to haul away the bodies.[34] Although a fairly modest UN force, with the authority and the means to stop it, could have done so, authorization was never given, primarily because of the United States. As Linda Melvern, whose book *A People Betrayed* reported the sickening details, said: "The Rwandan genocide should be the defining scandal of the presidency of Bill Clinton."[35]

Even more important, however, is the observation by moral philosopher Henry Shue, who said: "Any system of global governance" that allows such an event to occur "is ridiculous."[36] The revealing nature of the Rwanda massacre is even more telling when it is recalled that the construction of the new world order after World War II, especially the creation of the United Nations and its adoption of the Genocide Convention, was "guided by the principle: Never again." That is, the UN was to prevent genocide, such as that perpetrated by the Nazis against European Jews, from ever happening again. Nevertheless, "the world failed to react [in Rwanda] to the first indisputable genocide since that perpetrated against the Jews."[37]

Why are human rights still so unprotected, even to the point that genocide can still occur? The problem can be summarized in terms of a distinction, made by Richard Falk, between three logics: universalist logic, statist logic, and imperialist logic.[38] According to universalist logic, the rights of human beings in all places should be given equal protection. According to statist logic, states protect or violate human rights insofar as they believe that such behavior furthers their interests. The imperialist logic is the same except that the state in question rules an empire, which gives it not only a lot more interests but also distinctive interests, such as maintaining its "credibility," which can lead it to terrorize disobedient peoples to warn other peoples not to disobey. (This practice goes back at least to Roman crucifixions, one of which was the crucifixion of Jesus of Nazareth.)

Human rights have been so unprotected because they are at the mercy of the interests of very self-interested states. In the case of Rwanda, America had no material or geopolitical interests in the region, so the ridiculousness of the present world order, from the point of view of the universalist logic of human rights, was fully revealed. The massacre in Rwanda, furthermore, was simply an especially appalling exemplification of the fact that the rights enumerated in the Universal Declaration of Human Rights are massively violated in many parts of the world, as the annual reports of Amnesty International and Human Rights Watch make all too clear.

The basic problem is that the imperialist and statist logics are firmly embodied in the present world order, but the universalist logic is still disembodied. Although it is supposedly embodied in the UN, it is embodied there only rhetorically, because the UN was given no autonomy.[39] Accordingly, the UN intervenes only when its Security Council authorizes an intervention, and the five permanent members of the Security Council, which have veto power, are all imperial powers.[40] Only with the creation of a global democratic government, based on a global bill of rights and responsibilities, will the universalist logic of human rights finally be embodied in such a way that it can trump the logics of statism and imperialism. This is one reason, beyond ensuring survival itself, why global democracy is desirable.

Global Apartheid and the Right to Life

Another reason is that global democracy, and only global democracy, will allow us to overcome *global apartheid.* This name is increasingly being applied to the world's gap between rich and poor countries because of its stark similarities with the former South African regime.[41] In the planet as a whole, as it was in South Africa, one-sixth of the population, primarily light skinned, owns three-fourths of the resources and exercises military, political, economic, and cultural hegemony. There is democracy, affluence, leisure time, and consumer choice for the few, but oppression, poverty, long hours, and a struggle for subsistence for the many. The apartheid of the South African regime was morally condemned as a "crime against humanity."[42] But global apartheid is even worse, having greater inequality in income, healthcare, education, and mortality rate.[43] How can we not call it a crime against humanity?

This division between rich and poor countries originated in the colonial period, during which the European imperial powers restructured the economies of its colonies. The imposed trading arrangements involved what is called "asymmetrical interdependence," through which the European powers were enriched, and their colonies impoverished. In the twentieth century, the United States took primary control of this system in the disguised form of neocolonialism. Despite all the recent talk of "development," the asymmetry persists. Much more money flows from the poor to the rich countries than flows in the opposite direction, so that the gap between rich and poor countries continues to increase.[44] For example, the disparity in per capita income between America and the undeveloped nations in 1947 was about 13 to 1; by 1989 it was 60 to 1,[45] and today it is even greater.

As a result of this systemic creation of poverty, over half of the world's human beings now live in poverty, with many of them in *abject* poverty, which is the world's leading cause of death. We are right to be horrified by the Nazi regime's murder of some 12 million people. But we should be even more horrified by the fact that the global economy, over which America now presides, is responsible for 13 to 18 million deaths every year, most of which are due simply to a lack of adequate food, clean drinking water, and elementary healthcare.[46] This means that the American Empire is responsible, through a combination of indifference and deliberate policy, for at least 130 million easily preventable deaths every decade.[47] Becoming aware of this fact is so staggering, or at least should be, that even if there were no other reason, the need to overcome global apartheid, which is a *necessary* result of the present world order, should provide us with sufficient motivation for devoting ourselves wholeheartedly to the cause of global democracy. Over 100 million easily preventable deaths a decade is not acceptable "collateral damage."

The issue of adequate food and water is part of the issue of human rights. The unifying idea in the Universal Declaration of Human Rights is "the idea of a decent or minimally good life for all people."[48] Article 3 of the Universal Declaration specifically says that "everyone has the right to life." The right to a minimally decent life obviously involves the rights not to be murdered and not to be arbitrarily imprisoned, which we call civil and political rights. But it also includes the rights to adequate food and drinking water, which we call economic rights. Both kinds of rights belong to what Henry Shue calls "basic rights," because they are implicit in the very right to life. The basic economic rights are known as "subsistence rights," because they constitute the right to have enough simply to subsist, to stay alive. Basic rights, says Shue, constitute "the morality of the depths," because they specify "the line beneath which no one is to be allowed to sink."[49] In the present global economy, however, at least a billion people are allowed to slip below this line. Many of them are, in fact, pushed under.

In pointing at other countries, such as China and Cuba, for violating human rights, the US Government arbitrarily limits the idea of human rights to civil and political rights. But the United States, like most other countries, signed the UN's Covenant on Economic, Social and Cultural Rights, which is legally binding, and Article 11 of this Covenant says: "The States Parties to the present Covenant recognize the right of everyone to an adequate standard of living for himself and his family, including adequate food, clothing, and housing." So the United States is legally committed to honoring subsistence rights, which would require a radical change in the global economic system. But in the present world order, the United States can force other countries to live up to their commitments or punish them if they do not, but no one can force the United States to live up to its commitments, and no one can punish it when it refuses (except for terrorists).

In the global economy that is part and parcel of the American Empire, the economic rights of hundreds of millions of poor people are regularly denied in the name of the economic rights of the rich, which means that subsistence rights are trumped by luxury rights. As David Korten said, "property rights are too often used to legitimate denying others the right to live."[50] The right of the owners and CEOs of banks and corporations to have luxury automobiles, yachts, and villas around the world trumps the right of poor people to have food, clean water, and even minimal healthcare. The ethical system embodied in the present global economy, John McMurtry observed, "simply recognizes no right to live."[51] Even the quite conservative writer John Vincent said that "the whole international economic system in which we are all implicated" is morally illegitimate because of its "failure to provide subsistence rights."[52]

Besides being outraged by this morally illegitimate economic system, we should also be morally outraged that the global apartheid created by colonialism has been *deliberately* perpetuated by the *neo*colonial policies of the United States.[53] George Kennan's notorious State Department memo of 1947 cannot be too often repeated. In a top-secret memo, Kennan said:

> We have about 50% of the world's wealth, but only 6.3% of its population. . . . Our real task in the coming period is to devise a pattern of relationships which will permit us to maintain this position of disparity without positive detriment to our national security.[54]

Although Kennan considered himself a Christian, he was certainly not advocating the Golden Rule taught by Jesus. He was, instead, observing the Golden Rule practiced by plutocrats: Those with the gold make the rules. In any case, the United States got away with this policy for some 40 years, but the recent terrorism directed at America may have an element of that "positive detriment to our national security"—that "blowback"—which Kennan knew might be provoked by the policies he was advocating.

We need a global economic system that does not implicate us in crimes against humanity and that does not, by producing increasing misery in one part of the world, produce increasing blowback in another part. For this change to occur, the global economy needs to be regulated in terms of guidelines established by a global democratic government, which needs to include a global bill of rights and responsibilities that gives the subsistence rights of the poor priority over the luxury rights of the rich. We need an economic system that, rather than increasing global apartheid, begins overcoming it. This would mean reversing the direction taken by the global economy over the previous five centuries, the age of European imperialism, and especially the past century, the age of America's neocolonial empire. The only realistic basis for hope that this massive change of direction—this massive repentance—might occur is through the establishment of a global democratic government, through which the global economy can be regulated by principles promoting life for all rather than obscene wealth for the few and misery and death for the many.

Overcoming Economism

What John McMurtry called the "ethical system" embodied in the present global economy[55] is diametrically opposed to the basic principles of Christianity and other religions. This fact is illustrated by the global economy's failure to prevent a billion people from falling below "the line beneath which no one is to be allowed to sink," and its failure even to recognize a right to live. This complete opposition between religious ethical principles and the principles of the global economy is no surprise, because the global economy is the expression of an alternative religion, which from the viewpoint of Christianity and other religions can only be regarded as idolatrous.

John Cobb called this new religion "economism," which he defined as the belief "that primary devotion should be directed to the expansion of the economy."[56] What makes this belief religious is the idea that our "primary devotion" should be directed toward this task. As Luther pointed out, it is that which we worship—that to which we give our *primary* devotion—that is effectively our God. Cobb suggested that this religion has increasingly become the world's dominant religion since the middle of the twentieth century.[57] Rodney Dobell, who called this new religion "the religion of the market," agreed, saying:

> The hegemony achieved by this . . . economic religion—is remarkable; it has become a dogma of almost universal application, the dominant religion of our time, shoring up and justifying what would appear to be a patently inequitable status quo.[58]

Likewise, John McMurtry, calling it a "new world religion" and "new world theology," pointed out that it functions as the "deifier of the ruling order."[59]

This new theology, in other words, serves as an ideology to justify plutocracy, thereby creating complacency about the status quo, in spite of its massive inequities causing over a hundred million deaths every decade. As Nobel-prizewinning economist Amartya Sen has said: "What we do not need is global complacency in the iniquitous world of massive comfort and extreme misery in which we live."[60] But this is precisely the function of economic ideology, as explained by John Kenneth Galbraith in *The Culture of Contentment*.[61]

Creating and exporting this new world religion has been an integral part of that creation of the American Empire, as William Leach explained in *The Land of Desire*. It was in this land, Leach pointed out, that advertising became a specialized profession, being created by American big business near the end of the nineteenth century to manufacture desires for their manufactured goods. Saying that "Whoever has the power to project a vision of the good life and make it prevail has the most decisive power of all," Leach added:

> American business, after 1890, acquired such power and . . . in league with key institutions, began the transformation of American society into a society preoccupied with consumption, with comfort and bodily well-being,

with luxury, spending, and acquisition, with more goods this year than last, more next year than this.[62]

This process of manipulating desires on a large scale took a quantum leap after World War II, when the goal became more ambitious—to make consumerism the new religion. One advocate of this new religion, Victor Lebow, wrote:

> Our enormously productive economy . . . demands that we make consumption our way of life, that we convert the buying and use of goods into rituals, that we seek our spiritual satisfaction, our ego satisfaction, in consumption. . . . We need things consumed, burned up, worn out, replaced, and discarded at an ever increasing rate.[63]

Television soon became the primary medium through which corporations could shape the culture, especially in the US, where the average adult now sees an estimated 21,000 TV commercials a year, three-fourths of which are produced by the 100 largest corporations.[64] The impressionable minds of children, who from the age of 2 on may watch more TV than adults, are surely even more affected by this constant bombardment with images, which not only creates desires for specific products but also fosters a new spirituality. As Robert Bellah wrote: "That happiness is to be attained through limitless material acquisition is denied by every religion and philosophy known to humankind, but is preached incessantly by every American television set."[65]

This new gospel has not, of course, been preached only in America. As David Korten stated in *When Corporations Rule the World:*

> As global corporations reach out to the four corners of the earth, they bring with them not only established products and brand names but also their favored media and the sophisticated marketing methods by which they colonize every culture they touch.[66]

Television, which Korten called "the money world's most powerful tool of global cultural and ideological indoctrination," now reaches over 60 percent of the world's people, and global spending on advertising, which had reached $240 billion by 1989, had become almost twice that within another decade.[67] A 1997 book on the global media was appropriately subtitled *The New Missionaries of Corporate Capitalism.*[68] This missionary outreach has been more successful than any other in history. "The wildfire spread of the consumer lifestyle around the world," suggested Alan Durning, "marks the most rapid and fundamental change in day-to-day existence the human species has ever experienced." The tragic irony of all this, Durning added, is that although this transformation has been extremely successful in destroying the planet's life-support system, it has not brought any detectable increase in human happiness.[69]

Here we have the traditional features of idolatry: It does not bring happiness, because it leads to self-destruction, but it is tremendously seductive. By bringing into the picture the global media, which are owned by some of the world's largest corporations, which both support and are supported by the American Empire, we start to bring into view the full scope of the problem. The global airwaves belong in theory to the people rather than the corporations. They should be used to promote rather than destroy the common good. Instead of serving the tiny plutocratic class, they should be used to give people the information they need for informed democratic self-governance.[70] To bring about this massive change in the global media will require nothing less than the creation of a global democratic government, through which the people of the world can create media intended to promote the common good.

Morality & Patriotism

Global democracy is also the precondition for a reign of divine values on earth. I have here used the phrase "reign of divine values," instead of "the kingdom (or reign) of God," because the latter phrase is often taken to mean some state of absolute perfection. But Jesus, in speaking of a reign of God, did not seem to have in mind such a state. Like Isaiah 65, he seemed to mean simply a world ruled on the basis of justice and compassion—a world in which the economic system would not be used to impoverish people and take their land, in which every family had its daily bread so that babies did not die for want of food, in which people's homes were not destroyed by armies on the rampage, in which oppressive empires existed no more, in which all people could enjoy the fruits of God's good Earth. This is not an impossible vision. It is simply a vision of a world ordered in terms of moral principles. Such a vision could not be realized, of course, under the present world order, which is based on competition rather than cooperation, on promoting one's own good by defeating the good of others, and on using force to intimidate and even destroy those who get in one's way. But this vision could be realized through the creation of a global democracy.

Why would a global democracy provide a precondition—a necessary condition—for such a reign? We can begin negatively by asking why the other route for overcoming global anarchy, a global *Pax Americana*, cannot be expected to overcome the reign of power. Those who think it might may well agree, as did historian Andrew Bacevich in his 2004 book, *The American Empire*, that the history of American imperialism thus far has been anything but benign, so that the expectation of a benign *Pax Americana* cannot be based on past history. As illustrated in my 2018 book, *The American Trajectory*, they might say, nevertheless, that once America overcomes all its opponents so that a global peace finally exists, American leaders would likely institute a form of rule that is benign, perhaps even divine.

One problem with this expectation is that besides having no support in American history, it goes against a very widespread generalization about human nature, which has been summarized in Lord Acton's famous axiom: "Power tends to corrupt, and absolute power corrupts absolutely."[71] The central heresy of Marxism was its doctrine that there was one class, the proletariat, which was unaffected by sinful tendencies, so that it could be trusted with absolute power during a temporary "dictatorship of the proletariat." It was the resulting failure of many Marxist governments to build in checks and balances that lay behind their worst excesses. In the case of Stalin, absolute power within the Soviet Union clearly corrupted absolutely. And yet now the US government is seeking absolute power at the global level.

As we saw in chapter 5, Reinhold Niebuhr was surely correct in saying that only God can *perfectly* combine power and goodness. But this insight is compatible with the idea that a global democratic government could at least *approximate* the divine combination of power and goodness, thereby bringing about a far closer approximation to a reign of divine values than what we have now. A global democracy could achieve such an approximation, because the collective body, being from all regions of the world, could partly make up for the defects in each individual. That is, the ignorance of each individual about most of the world except for his or her own region would be corrected by the knowledge of the representatives from those regions. The indifference that each representative has toward the welfare of peoples from most parts of the world would be made up for by the sympathy possessed by the representative from these parts. The partisan biases of each representative could be balanced by the biases of the others. The collective body could, therefore, embody firsthand knowledge of the facts, along with real sympathy for and benevolence toward the various affected parties in the various regions.[72]

At first glance, it would seem that the idea of giving supreme power to a global government would also run afoul of Acton's dictum. If a global government had sufficient power to enforce its rulings on the various states, would this not be at least *virtually* absolute power? And if Acton's dictum is correct, should we not expect the global government to become absolutely corrupt, or at least virtually so?

To see why this does not follow, we need to see a qualification that was implicit in Acton's dictum. Acton would not have believed that absolute power would *always* corrupt because, as a good Catholic, he surely believed that God had absolute power without believing that God was made corrupt by such power. The difference between God and any creature, including any creaturely institution,[73] is that creatures have limited sympathies, so that their interests in the welfare of the rest of the world are quite limited. God's sympathy, by contrast, is all-inclusive, so that God's "self-interest," if we wish to put it this way, is identical with God's interest in the welfare of the whole world and all its creatures. This is, in any case, the idea of God presupposed in the present work. In God, and in God alone, self-interest (promoting one's own interests) and altruism (promoting the interests of others) coincide.

But in our case, our self-interest is often very exclusive and hence, as we put it, "selfish." Promoting our own self-interest usually means acting in a way that involves indifference to, or even active opposition to, the welfare of most other creatures. With this distinction between God and human beings in mind, we can see that Acton's dictum, spelled out more fully, should read: "Human beings, because of their limited sympathies and hence selfish interests, tend to be corrupted by power; and they are corrupted absolutely by absolute power." Although this statement is not as pithy and catchy, it states the point more fully by bringing out the crucial fact: that it is because of our limited sympathies that we cannot be trusted with unlimited power.

However, based on this same reasoning, there is one kind of human institution—a global democratic government—in which supreme power would not necessarily corrupt. This is the case because a global democratic government's interests would by definition be all-inclusive.[74] It would be mandated by charter to serve the good of human civilization as a whole. It would have a bill of rights and responsibilities, in which the rights and responsibilities of all individuals and nations are explained. And it would have representatives from all peoples in its legislative, executive, and judicial branches and in its police forces. Insofar as we think of God's central feature as love—impartial sympathetic love for all creatures and hence active good will towards all creatures—a global democratic government would provide at least the necessary condition for the human potential to be the *imago dei* finally to be actualized. Put in other language, it would provide us with the best possibility for fulfilling the basic religious urge to live in terms of an *imitatio dei*, because in global democracy at its best, self-interest and altruism would be identical. Insofar as that is actually the case, a global government's power would be used to heal rather than to destroy because it, being impartially concerned for the welfare of all its peoples, would always be working for the general good.

Such a government could, therefore, meet the need, seen by the early Niebuhr, to transcend our anarchical world order, in which disputes based on conflicting perspectives are settled by brute force. "There must be an organizing centre," Niebuhr said, that can "arbitrate conflicts from a more impartial perspective than is available to any party of a given conflict."[75] If force is to be redemptive rather than destructive, he added, "it is an absolute prerequisite that it be exerted by an agency that is impartial."[76] Niebuhr in these passages did not demand perfection, only a power that is exercised with far greater impartiality than possessed by any of the competing parties. We could hope for such impartiality from, and only from, a global democratic government.[77]

An obvious objection to this vision of how enlightened democratic rule could be is that few if any national democratic governments have approached this ideal. The answer to this objection is that all such governments have been more or less corrupted by at least two factors. On the one hand, as discussed earlier, they have been corrupted by the power of money. Instead of decisions being made on the basis of the best arguments about what would best promote the common good, decisions have been made to please special interests. Also all national democracies have existed within the anarchical, competitive system of states, with its "war of all against all." In this situation, the policies of a state have often been directed less at promoting the common good of humanity than at protecting the existence of the state and enhancing its power *vis-à-vis* other states. When these two corrupting influences are combined, enormous distortions are likely, as illustrated by the enormous portion of the US budget directed toward the purchase of weapons produced by giant corporations that have made huge political contributions. In a global democratic government shielded from the influence of money and other forms of bribery, the decisions might really be such as to promote the general good.[78]

One way to put this qualification of Acton's dictum is that the idea of "exceptionalism," upon which the American self-image has been based, is not wholly wrong. There has always been one exception to the general principle that power tends to corrupt, as noted above, and that is God. It is the coincidence of self-interest and altruism, we have seen, that lies behind this divine exceptionalism. And there could in principle be a human organization that could approximate that coincidence. American exceptionalism, in presupposing these ideas, has not been wrong. But where it has been wrong, and grossly and perversely so (as shown in *The American Trajectory*), has been in the conceit that America itself, very much one competing power among others with extremely partial and partisan interests, could be that approximation. This American exceptionalism has been this country's primal intellectual sin. It is embodied throughout American history, from the theology of "manifest destiny" to the slogan that "what is good for America is good for the world" to the current school of "benign American imperialism," according to which American interests coincide with American ideals, which promote democracy, human rights, and self-determination for all peoples. All of these embodiments of American exceptionalism seek to camouflage the fact that human nature does not, simply by being stamped "made in America," become magically transformed into a finite version of the divine coincidence between self-interest and universal altruism. If the good, as the early Niebuhr said, is "always the harmony of the whole on various levels," whereas "evil is always the assertion of some self-interest without regard to the whole,"[79] American foreign policy has been evil, not good. The American Empire neither has been, nor will be, the exception to Acton's dictum.

But if human nature is so self-interested, how can we hope that human beings could create a form of universal self-rule that would embody justice? Here we need to return to the first part of Niebuhr's dictum, which speaks of our "capacity for justice." The contrast between this and our "inclination to injustice" depends upon a distinction between two contrasting stances: contemplation and action. *In contemplation*, Niebuhr said, it is possible for us to rise to a high level of disinterested impartiality, in which we can see what would be just in some situation for all affected parties. The self *in action*—one that is actually participating in the historical process, with its claims and counterclaims—will inevitably lose this impartiality, becoming one egoistic combatant among others. The fact that our practical reason is intertwined with our "vitality," including our will to power, Niebuhr said, "guarantees that egoistic purposes will be pursued with all vital resources which an individual or collective will may control."[80] This has been at least as true of America as it has been of any other participant in the historical process. But this fact about the self in action is compatible with the recognition that the self in contemplation can rise to a high level of disinterested impartiality. The ideological bias that would still remain could, furthermore, be overcome in contemplative conferences involving selves from various regions, as the biases in each perspective would cancel each other out. We can, therefore, have a realistic hope that a global constitutional convention, based on numerous preparatory conferences and documents, could construct a constitution that would truly embody the principles of justice.

Why Global Democracy May Be Possible

It could be, of course, that global democracy is both necessary for survival and otherwise desirable for many reasons—and yet impossible to create. There have, indeed, been many reasons given for thinking it to be impossible, but the most formidable in today's world is simply the likelihood that the richest and most powerful states would prevent it. Is it possible to imagine a route through which global democracy might be created?

A Common Cause for Moral NGOs

Reflection about such a route can begin by reflecting on the suggestion, made recently by a number of thinkers, that in spite of America's claim to be the only superpower, there is actually a second superpower: global civil society. If the people of the world were united behind a cause to which they were passionately committed, they would indeed constitute a force against which the US superpower, equipped to wage military and economic warfare, might be relatively helpless. But at present global civil society has no such cause. A remarkable phenomenon of recent decades, to be sure, is the growth of thousands of NGOs (nongovernmental organizations) committed to moral goals. But these goals are various, with some moral NGOs working against nuclear weapons, others against war or some specific war, others against the weaponization of space, others for human rights, others for workers' rights, others for biodiversity, others for population control, others against global warming, others for economic democracy, others against corporate welfare; others against the IMF, the World Bank, and the WTO; others for a strengthened UN, and so on. Some of these NGOs have joined together in what has been, if misleadingly, called the "anti-globalization movement," but for the most part each NGO focuses on its own concern, working independently or at most in conjunction with other NGOs working on the same concern. As such, these NGOs are usually so out-funded and out-organized by the interests they oppose that their victories are seldom and, when they do come, fleeting. Global civil society at present constitutes nothing approaching superpower status.

Global civil society could become a powerful force, however, if the majority of its moral NGOs became united behind a single cause. Global democracy could become that cause. It is, in fact, the most logical candidate for the common cause. One of the most important features of the project for global democracy is that it is the solution to a wide range of problems, such as the war-nuclearism-imperialism-terrorism complex, global climate change, civil and political rights, global apartheid and subsistence rights, and economism. With these and all other issues of global scope, a good case can be made that an adequate solution will be unlikely apart from the creation of global democracy. Insofar as this case is convincingly made, activists for global causes will come to realize that, whatever their cause, it is a lost cause without global democracy.[81]

They will realize, therefore, that the practical thing to do would be to work for their own cause while working simultaneously, in conjunction with many other organizations, for global democracy. If a majority of the moral NGOs of the world join forces, combining their money, expertise, and sheer numbers, they will be able to wield tremendous influence. Out of these reflections comes a recommendation: *Moral NGOs of the world unite! You have nothing to lose but your impotence.*

A Common Cause for the Religious NGOs

Even when combined, however, the number of people and especially the financial and organizational resources of the moral NGOs would still be tiny in comparison with that of giant corporations and the governments supporting them. But there is another part of global civil society that is *not* tiny—the religious traditions of the world, which can be called religious NGOs. If we combine the adherents of Buddhism, Christianity, Hinduism, Islam, and Judaism, we have over 4 billion of the world's peoples. Adding the Chinese religious traditions and the indigenous traditions around the world would raise the number to well over 5 billion. If a significant percentage of the religious NGOs became committed to the cause of global democracy, we would have a significant global movement.

But is this conceivable? Are not the religions of the world too different to join forces? Does not religious and cultural diversity prevent a common global ethic? The idea that it does has been, in fact, one of the major arguments for considering a global democratic government impossible.[82] However, although it is true that the various religions are different from each other, some of them *radically* different,[83] they share a set of moral values—moral values, furthermore, that are diametrically opposed to the values in terms of which the world is now governed. The Abrahamic religions—Judaism, Christianity, and Islam—all share moral codes that say, for example (in updated translations):

Do not covet your neighbor's oil or water.

Do not steal your neighbors's oil or water.

Do not murder your neighbors in order to steal their oil or water.

Do not bear false witness against your neighbors—falsely calling them "terrorists"—in order to justify murdering them in order to steal their oil or water.

The values of the present global order are equally opposed by the moral codes of Buddhism, Hinduism, Confucianism, Taoism, Zoroastrianism, and the various indigenous traditions. They are also opposed by moral Marxism.[84] As Hans Küng has pointed out, most if not all the traditions affirm some version of what Christians have called the golden rule—at least in its negative formulation, which scholars have called the "silver rule": Do not do to others what you would not want done to you.[85] And yet that is precisely what the present world order, based on the rule of force, rather than law, allows.

A helpful way of thinking about this issue can be derived from Michael Walzer's little book, *Thick and Thin*. In earlier writings, Walzer's concern with difference and particularity had seemed to lead him to a relativistic position. In the debate between the "cosmopolitans," who affirm a cosmopolitan or universal morality, and the "communitarians," who emphasize the distinctive ethos of each nation or cultural tradition, he was placed firmly in the latter camp. He was read as denying any universal moral principles. But in *Thick and Thin* he argued that every thick, particularist morality has within it "the makings of a thin and universalist morality."[86]

He now affirmed, in other words, a position that could be called "cosmopolitan communitarianism" or "communitarian cosmopolitanism." Such a position could provide the background for a federated global system that, while affirming universal moral standards, recognizes that people, as Walzer said, live in terms of their own thick traditions. This position, far from implying, as pure cosmopolitanism seems to do, a homogenized world, provides a basis for resisting the homogenization being rather ruthlessly carried out in the "globalization."

Walzer pointed out that, because the world's various peoples live in terms of their own thick traditions, which are quite different from each other, the thin, universalist morality usually becomes apparent "only on special occasions," especially when there is "the sense of a common enemy."[87] In calling this universalist morality "thin," Walzer did not mean that it is unimportant. Indeed, he said:

> The opposite is more likely true: this is morality close to the bone. There isn't much that is more important than 'truth' and 'justice,' minimally understood. The minimal demands that we make on one another are, when denied, repeated with passionate insistence. In moral discourse, thinness and intensity go together.[88]

It is the recognition that we share this passionate commitment to such basic principles as truth and justice that is evoked when we become aware of a common enemy.

The common enemy of all the world's religious traditions is the present world order, with its plutocracy and imperialism based on its anarchy. What is needed now is only the "and responsibilities" that this is so; indeed, this sense has been rapidly forming in recent years.[89] Indeed, at least most of these traditions could probably condemn the present world order as demonic. Although when representatives of these various traditions look at each other in terms of their specifically theological and metaphysical beliefs, they may be convinced that their differences are more important then their commonalities, when they look at each other in relation to the plutocratic imperialism of today's world order, they will increasingly see the set of core moral beliefs that they all hold in common. On this basis, representatives of these traditions could fashion a global bill of rights and responsibilities for a global constitution.

When we think of religion and ethics today, we often conjure up images of religious fundamentalists wanting to impose their highly particular moral code on everyone else. The attempt to implement that desire, however, would go against one of the fundamental points of the thin morality that is common to everyone. Walzer calls this fundamental point *the principle of self-determination*. It implies that people, as members of communities, have, in Walzer's words, "the basic right *to govern themselves* (in accordance with their own political ideas)—insofar as they can decently do that."[90] In other words, aside from the thin, quite abstract moral principles that the representatives at a constitutional convention would agree upon as universally valid, no other principles would be imposed on anyone. Each community would be free to govern itself in accordance with the political ideas that arise from its own tradition—with the caveat that it do so "decently." This qualification, about *decent* self-governance, means that a global constitution should allow communities to govern themselves in terms of their own norms as long as those norms do not violate any of the thin, universal moral principles that were included in the universal bill of rights and responsibilities by mutual consent.

We can see, therefore, that the religious passion brought by members of the various religious NGOs of the world need not work against the need for a common front committed to effecting a transition from today's anarchical, plutocratic, imperialist world order to a democratic world order. In this new world order, the system of settling differences by the threat and use of force would be replaced by legal pacifism, also called "Einsteinian pacifism," in which disputes are settled by appeal to impartial judges. The principle of "might makes right" will be replaced by having might support right. The plutocrat's golden rule, according to which those with the gold make the rules, will be replaced by laws based on the religious traditions' silver rule, according to which one should not do to others what one would not want done to oneself.

Devising laws that exemplify this tradition will not, it should be emphasized, be terribly difficult. None of us want to be deprived of adequate food and water, to be arbitrarily imprisoned and tortured, to have our land or other property stolen, to have our towns and villages strafed and bombed, to have our homes demolished by tanks, to have our family members raped or mutilated by land mines, or to be persecuted for our religious beliefs. Such a world order could, accordingly, be passionately sought by members of all religious traditions, whatever their other differences, and regardless of whether they belong to the fundamentalist, conservative, liberal, or radical branch of their own tradition.

These reflections lead to the following recommendation: *Religions of the world unite! You have nothing to lose but your impotence.* The Abrahamic religions—Judaism, Christianity, and Islam—are not unique in having a vision of a form of human society that is based on divine rather than demonic values. Such a vision is found in most, if not all, religious traditions. But thus far, with a few temporary exceptions, such societies have not appeared. When religious leaders have called for the creation of a society that reflected their tradition's principles, the Political Realists have told them that they are impractical dreamers, utopians. Only in heaven will a society based on such principles be possible. In the world as it is, the Realists have insisted, those principles would lead to the society's destruction. And they have been right. In the world of anarchical civilization, the war of all against all requires that each society, if it is to thrive or even survive in this competitive situation, must be organized on the basis of quite other principles. But now, with the shrinking of the world brought about by the modern technologies of communication and transportation, it is finally possible to overcome this anarchical situation. By uniting to bring this about, the religions will have created the precondition for societies that at least approximate their long-standing dreams.

"The great social ideal for religion," said Whitehead, "is that it should be the common basis for the unity of civilization. In that way it justifies its insight beyond the transient clash of brute forces."[91] From the perspective of the dominant way of thinking about religion in the modern world, Whitehead's suggestion is absurd. From this perspective, religion is the source of mutual hostility, not unity. And of course this has all too often been the case. Whitehead himself was well aware of this, preceding his statement with the rhetorical question: "Must 'religion' always remain as a synonym for 'hatred'?"

The suggestion made here is that religion can become a source of unity if we—in response to the common enemy of the ideals of all the religions—focus on the fact that we do have these ideals in common, along with the conviction that we have them in common because they are inherent in the nature of things,[92] this being a reflection of the religious nature of the universe. This approach, which is in line with Whitehead's own thought,[93] would mean that all the religions would be agreeing that a global democracy, insofar as it exemplified the basic moral principles common to all the traditions, would be a reign of divine values.

The exemplification, as the word "insofar" indicates, would be a matter of degree. But a world order based on a global democratic government would, even if far from perfect, be a vast improvement over the present world order. Insofar as the world order really did embody those common moral principles, the common dream of the various religious traditions—for a form of human social life that reflects divinely rooted moral principles—would finally be realized. The various religious traditions, therefore, have religious as well as strictly moral reasons to unite behind this cause.

Implicit in this vision is a middle position between two extremes. One extreme is the "political liberalism" that advocates a purely secular state.[94] The other extreme involves the advocacy of a full-fledged theocracy based on a particular tradition, such as an Islamic state based on the *shari'a* or a "Christian America" based on the Bible as interpreted by Christian Fundamentalists.[95] In contrast with the first extreme, this middle position argues that a state cannot be fully separated from religion because, as recent moral thought has shown, even basic moral principles cannot be justified apart from some sort of religious view of reality.[96] In contrast with the second extreme, this middle position says that the quest for a theocracy in the traditional sense is misguided, both because such so-called theocracies tend to become more demonic than divine and because they are not necessary in order to overcome what they justifiably oppose. That is, to overcome a situation in which, say, a basically Muslim country is being economically exploited and culturally corrupted, there is no need for a theocracy that imposes moral and religious customs of some prior society. What is needed is only a government based on the basic moral principles that are shared by all the religious traditions. Because a global government based on those principles would *ipso facto* be based on the fundamental moral principles of Islam, it would be an Islamic government. But because these principles are also the basic moral principles of Buddhism, Christianity, Confucianism, Hinduism, and Judaism, it would equally support a Buddhist, a Christian, a Confucian, a Hindu, or a Jewish government.

However, whereas the religious NGOs can supply great numbers of people, motivated by religious passion, to work for this cause, they will generally not have the various kinds of theoretical knowledge and practical wisdom, based on experience, to organize the kind of massive global movement that will be required to turn global democracy, which is now only a vague ideal, into a concrete proposal and then a practical reality. But the moral NGOs, discussed earlier, do. Having long been battling with governments, they have, between themselves, access to massive amounts of ecological, political, economic, financial, historical, cultural, legal and other kinds of knowledge that will be needed both to make the case for a global government and to assist with the creation of an effective and acceptable constitution for it. Some of these kinds of knowledge are ones that can be provided by religious as well as moral NGOs, such as knowledge about effecting reconciliation between erstwhile enemies.

In any case, in light of the complementary strengths of the

religious and the moral NGOs, combined with the massiveness of the project before us, our inclusive motto must be: *Religious and moral NGOs of the world unite! You have nothing to lose but your impotence. And you have everything to gain.*[97]

To fellow Christians in America, I would add that it is especially incumbent on us to take a leading role in this movement. Modern imperialism has been primarily a Christian phenomenon. The British Empire and now the American Empire have been created by countries regarding themselves as primarily Christian. And it is primarily during the period since the second world war, when the US became especially dominant, that imperialism has come to be seen as a threat to the very existence of civilization. Furthermore, whatever the restrictions on our civil and political freedoms that have been enacted in recent times, we still have far more freedom than do most of the peoples of the world. Finally, as the citizens of the global empire, we have, like the inhabitants of Rome, been the primary beneficiaries of imperial policies, even if they have been carried out largely without our knowledge. Given all of these facts, combined with our new awareness that our religion began with a vision of a radical alternative to empire (as discussed in my 2019 book, *The Christian Gospel for Americans*), we need to live out the implications of our fidelity to the God of Jesus by participating fully in a worldwide movement to democratize human civilization.

I would, in fact, suggest that it is time for Christians in America to consider whether the situation created by American imperialism creates a *status confessionis*, a confessional situation. In the twentieth century, Nazism and South African Apartheid led to such situations. In Germany in 1934, a year after the rise to power of the Nazi Party, the movement known as *Deutsche Christen*, "German Christians," were supporting the program of the National Socialists because they believed it would bring Germany the greatness that it deserved. But a number of theologians, led by Karl Barth and Dietrich Bonhoeffer, led a movement of Confessing Christians who said, in their famous Barmen Declaration, that this support for National Socialism violated basic principles of the Christian faith, thereby creating a confessional situation. Later in the century, some Christian bodies decided that the system of apartheid in South Africa could not be a matter of indifference. One such body was the Lutheran World Federation in its worldwide assembly in 1977. "Under normal circumstances," it declared, "Christians may have different opinions in political questions." But the system of apartheid in South Africa, it continued, is "so perverted and oppressive" that this situation "constitutes a *status confessionis.*" The Christian faith required, therefore, that "churches would publicly and unequivocally reject the existing apartheid system" and "work for changes."[98]

I suggest that Christians in America now need to decide whether an examination of the facts of the American Empire, in conjunction with a reexamination of our Christian faith and American ideals rooted in it, should lead us "publicly and unequivocally" to reject the present world order and "work for changes"—with the primary changes being those that would be involved in the transformation of the present world order, which allows for war, imperialism, and plutocracy, into a global democracy.

ENDNOTES

PREFACE

1. David Ray Griffin, "Whitehead and Niebuhr on God, Man, and the World," *Journal of Religion* 52 (April 1973), 149–75.

CHAPTER ONE

1. Although the use of the terms "nations" and "nation-states" to refer to countries or states is problematic, I have used these terms interchangeably, in agreement with widespread practice.

2. According to Hedley Bull's *The Anarchical Society: A Study of Order in World Politics* (London: Macmillan, 1977), 46, this expression was made famous—by which he means among people conversant with the study of international politics—by G. Lowes Dickinson's *The International Anarchy, 1904–14* (London: Allen and Unwin, 1926).

3. F. H. Hinsley, for example, protested against the tendency to identify "the attribute of sovereignty with the possession by the state of freedom to act as it chooses instead of with the absence over and above the state of a superior authority" (*Sovereignty*

[Basic *Books,* 1966]), 226).

4. Michael Ross Fowler and Julie Marie Bunck, *Law, Power, and the Sovereign State: The Evolution and Application of the Concept of Sovereignty* (University Park: Pennsylvania State University Press, 1995), 4.

5. Jean Bethke Elshtain, *New Wine and Old Bottles: International Politics and Ethical Discourse* (Notre Dame University Press, 1998), 12.

6. Jean Bodin, *Six Books of the Commonwealth* (Macmillan, 1955), 32.

7. In developing this theory of sovereignty, however, Bodin drew on sovereign theory that had been developed by defenders of the papacy as rightly embodying the plenitude of power (see Elshtain, *New Wine and Old Bottles,* 46–47 n. 11, citing Anthony Black, *Monarchy and Community: Political Ideas in the Later Conciliar Controversy, 1430–1450* (Cambridge University Press, 1970), 80–81, a fact that further underscores the theological roots of the theory.

8. Fowler and Bunck, *Law, Power, and the Sovereign State,* 4.

9. Tomaz Mastnak, "Fascists, Liberals, and Anti-Nationalism," in Richard Caplan and John Feffer, eds., *Europe's New Nationalism: States and Minorities in Conflict* (Oxford: Oxford University Press, 1996), 62.

10. Bull, *The Anarchical Society,* 31.

11. Although it can be said that this idea of external sovereignty, with its proscription against intervention, was being implicitly accepted somewhat earlier, credit for explicitly extending Bodin's view of sovereignty to the external relations of states is usually given to the eighteenth-century Swiss jurist Emmerich de Vattel (author of *The Law of Nations or the Principles of Natural Law Applied to the Conduct and to the Affairs of Nations and of Sovereigns*). Vattel had, however, been heavily influenced on this point by Christian Wolff.

12. Gene M. Lyons and Michael Mastanduno, eds., *Beyond Westphalia?*

State Sovereignty and International Intervention (Baltimore: John Hopkins University Press 1995), 5.

13. Thomas G. Weiss and Jarat Chopra, "Sovereignty Is No Longer Sacrosanct: Codifying Humanitarian Intervention," *Ethics and International Affairs* (March 1992): 95–117.

14. Christopher Layne, "Kant or Cant: The Myth of the Democratic Peace," in Michael E. Brown et al., eds. *The Perils of Anarchy: Contemporary Realism and International Security* (Cambridge, MA: MIT Press, 1995), 293.

15. When I use the term "realism" for this political school of thought, I always capitalize it (except when quoting authors who do not), writing "Political Realism" or simply "Realism," partly as a reminder that there may in some cases be a distinction between what Realism holds and what is truly realistic.

16. Michael E. Brown et al., eds., *The Perils of Anarchy*, ix.

17. John Mearsheimer, "The False Promise of International Relations," Brown et al., eds. *The Perils of Anarchy*, 332–76, at 333. The phrase "government over governments" was quoted from Inis Claude, Jr., *Swords Into Plowshares: The Problems and Progress of International Organization,* 4th edition (New York: Random House, 1971), 14.

18. David Held, *Democracy and the Global Order: From the Modern State to Cosmopolitan Governance* (Stanford: Stanford University Press, 1995), 74–75.

CHAPTER TWO

1. This chapter's survey of ideas and developments is limited to the West, the tradition in which the League of Nations and the United Nations were created.

2. Quoted in Cornelius F. Murphy, Jr., *Theories of World Governance: A Study in the History of Ideas* (Washington, DC: Catholic University of America Press, 1999), 203.

3. Murphy, *Theories of World Governance,* 5.

4. Lord Acton, *Essays,* ed. Rufus F. Fears, vol. 2 (Carmel, IN: Liberty Classics, 1985), 383.

5. Sylvester John Hemleben, *Plans for World Peace through Six Centuries* (University of Chicago Press, 1943), 25–30.

6. Thomas Hobbes, *Leviathan* (New York: Liberal Arts Press, 1958), 108, 169.

7. Hugo Grotius, *De Jure Belli ac Pacis* ("The Rights of War and Peace"), in *Peace Projects of the Seventeenth Century* (New York: Garland, 1972), 35.

8. Jean-Jacques Rousseau, *Emile,* trans. Barbara Foxley (New York: Everyman's Library, 1974), 458. A more recent critic, B.V.A. Röling, has said: "The enormous popularity of Grotius' doctrine becomes comprehensible when we recognize that in theory it could gratify the high-minded ... while in practice it did not restrict in any way the endeavour to subjugate the non-European peoples to European authority" ("Are Grotius' Ideas Obsolete in an Expanded World," in *Hugo Grotius and International Relations,* ed. Hedley Bull et al. [Oxford: Clarendon, 1992], 281–99, at 295, 297).

9. Murphy, *Theories of World Governance,* 15, 30.

10. Here I am summarizing the discussion in Murphy, *Theories,* 28–31.

11. Murphy, *Theories of World Governance,* 31.

12. Hemleben, *Plans for World Peace through Six Centuries,* 11–19.

13. For the sources of these points, see Hemleben, *Plans for World Peace,* 75–77, and Grace Roosevelt, *Reading Rousseau in the Nuclear Age* (Templeton University Press, 1990), 27–31, 100–04.

14. Rousseau apparently believed that some such plan might eventually be adopted. (Grace Roosevelt argued that previous interpreters of Rousseau, including Stanley Hoffman and F.H. Hinsley, had wrongly concluded, due to the fact that the pages of *The State of War* were out of order, that he was pessimistic about the

possibility of ending war. See *Reading Rousseau in the Nuclear Age,* 10, 66, referring to her essay "A Reconstruction of Rousseau's Fragments on the State of War," *History of Political Thought* 8 [Summer 1987]: 225–44). One basis for Rousseau's optimism was his distinction between self-love (*amour de soi*), which is natural, and selfish love (*amour propre*), which is socially created. It is the latter that motivates war, said Rousseau *(A Project of Perpetual Peace: Rousseau's Essay,* trans. by Edith M. Nuttall, with an Introduction by G. Lowes Dickinson [London: Richard Cobden-Sanderson, 1917], 30–31). Previous philosophers—especially Hobbes, with his belief that all people have "a perpetual and restless desire of power after power that ceases only in death" (*Leviathan*, 87)—have misunderstood the state of nature, said Rousseau. "Speaking continually of need, avarice, oppression, desires, and pride, [they] have carried over to the state of nature ideas they had acquired in society" (Rousseau, *Discourse on the Origins of Inequality,* Preface). Accordingly, said Roosevelt, when Rousseau declared in *The State of War* that "it is not in natural man that one finds the great propensities for war," he meant that war "is an artificial consequence of conventional politics," not "a natural consequence of innate aggressiveness" (Roosevelt, *Reading Rousseau in the Nuclear Age,* 58).

15. Roosevelt, *Reading Rousseau in the Nuclear Age,* 104.

16. In one of his last books, in fact, Kant said that the "task of establishing a universal and lasting peace is not just a part of the theory of right within the limits of pure reason, but its entire ultimate purpose." See "The Metaphysics of Morals," as printed in Hans Reiss, ed., *Kant: Political Writings,* 2nd ed. (Cambridge University Press, 1991), 131–75, at 174.

17. "Perpetual Peace: A Philosophical Sketch," as published in 1796, is an enlarged edition of a version released in 1795.

18. Immanuel Kant, "Perpetual Peace," in Reiss, ed., *Kant: Political Writings,* 93–130, at 104.

19. Kant, "The Metaphysics of Morals," 165.

20. Kant, "The Idea for a Universal History with a Cosmopolitan Purpose," as printed in Reiss, ed., *Kant: Political Writings,* 41–53, at 48–49.

21. Kant, "On the Common Saying: 'This May Be True in Theory, but It Does not Apply in Practice," as printed in Reiss, ed., *Kant: Political Writings,* 61–92, at 90.

22. Kant, "On the Common Saying," in Reiss, *Kant: Political Writing,* 90.

23. Kant, "On the Common Saying." in Reiss, *Kant: Political Writing,* 91–92.

24. See Hidemi Suganami, *The Domestic Analogy and World Order Proposals* (Cambridge: Cambridge University Press, 1989).

25. Kant, "Perpetual Peace," in Reiss, *Kant's Political Writings,* 105.

26. Kant, "Perpetual Peace," in Reiss, *Kant's Political Writings,* 105.

27. Kant, "On the Common Saying," 92. Writers who are hostile to the idea of a global government often suggest that Kant himself said that such a government would degenerate into "soulless despotism." However, what Kant actually said, after speaking of the necessity for a "federal union to prevent hostilities breaking out," is that even the continuation of the present system would be preferable to "an amalgamation of the separate nations under a single power which has overruled the rest and created a universal monarchy" ("The Metaphysics of Morals," in Reiss, ed., *Kant: Political Writings,* 113). It is this type of world government—one that had been achieved by conquest—that would be a "soulless despotism."

28. Hemleben, *Plans for World Peace through Six Centuries,* 106–08.

29. James Lorimer, *The Institutes of the Law of Nations,* 2 vols. (Edinburgh: E. Blackwood, 1883–84).

30. Murphy, *Theories of World Governance,* 71–72, 139.

31. Lorimer, *The Institutes of the Law of Nations,* vol. 2, 273.

32. Lorimer, *The Institutes of the Law of Nations,* vol. 2, 273, 279.

33. Murphy, *Theories of World Governance,* 73, 76.

34. *Nicholas Murray Butler's The International Mind,* ed. Charles F. Howlett (Information Age Publishing and Charles F. Howlett, 2013), 8.

35. Lassa Oppenheim, *The Future of International Law* (London: Clarendon Press, 1921).

36. I have here followed Murphy's summary in *Theories of World Governance,* 78.

37. Murphy, *Theories of World Governance,* 79.

38. Carsten Holbraad, *The Concert of Europe: A Study in German and British International Theory 1815–1914* (London: Longman, 1970), 2, 3.

39. Hemleben, *Plans for World Peace through Six Centuries,* 186.

40. René Albrecht-Carrié, ed., *The Concert of Europe* (New York: Walker, 1968), 11.

41. Albrecht-Carrié, *The Concert of Europe* 22, 241; Holbraad, *The Concert of Europe,* 2.

42. F. S. Northedge, *The League of Nations: Its Life and Times 1920–1946* (New York: Holmes and Meier, 1986), 3.

43. David Mitrany, *The Functional Theory of Politics* (St. Martin's Press, 1976), 4–5, quoted in Hidemi Suganami, *The Domestic Analogy.*

CHAPTER THREE

1. F. S. Northedge, *The League of Nations: Its Life and Times 1920–1946* (New York: Holmes and Meier, 1986), 3.

2. David Mitrany, *The Functional Theory of Politics* (New York: St. Martin's Press, 1975), 4–5; quoted in Hidemi Suganami, "Reflections on the Domestic Analogy: The Case of Bull, Beitz and Linklater," *Review of International Studies* 2, no. 2 (April 1986).

3. George Keeton, *National Sovereignty and International Order*

(London: Peace Book Company, [1923] 1939), 68.

4. Lassa Oppenheim, *International Law*, ed. R.F. Roxburgh, 3rd edition, vol. 2 (London: Longmans, Green, 1920), 291–94.

5. Woodrow Wilson: "Address delivered at the First Annual Assemblage of the League to Enforce Peace: 'American Principles,'" 27 May 1916, https://www.presidency.ucsb.edu/documents/address-delivered -the-first-annual-assemblage-the-league-enforce-peace-american -principles.

6. Woodrow Wilson: "Address to the Senate of the United States: "A World League for Peace," 22 January 1917, https://www. presidency.ucsb.edu/documents/address-the-senate-the-united -states-world-league-for-peace.

7. Senator Henry Cabot Lodge, in an address to the League to Enforce Peace, 27 May 1916, quoted in Alan Cranston, *The Killing of the Peace* (New York: Viking, 1945), 1.

8. Theodore Roosevelt, *America and the World War* (N.p.: CreateSpace Independent Publishing Platform [1915], 2016), 144.

9. Northedge, *The League of Nations*, 1.

10. Jean-Jacques Rousseau, *A Lasting Peace through the Federation of Europe and The State of War* (1756), trans. Charles Edwyn Vaughan (London: Constable and Co., 1917).

11. George Bernard Shaw "Introduction," in Leonard S. Woolf, *International Government* (London: Fabian Society, 1915), xvi, xvii.

12. Leonard S. Woolf, *International Government* (New York: Garland Publishing, [1915] 1971), 4–5, 111, 125.

13. Woolf, *International Government*, 105.

14. Woolf, *International Government*, 118.

15. Woolf, *International Government*, 143, 372.

16. Woolf, *International Government*, 372.

17. Stephen J. Stearns, "Introduction," in Woolf, *International Government*, 19.

18. Wilson: "Address to the Senate of the United States."

19. Northedge, *The League of Nations,* 49, 53, 44.

20. Wilson: "Address to the Senate of the United States."

21. Northedge, *The League of Nations,* 53.

22. The Senate failed to ratify in spite of the prediction by Senator Joseph Randsdall that "if the League of Nations be not adopted…, within a few years—ten or twenty years at most—another war far greater than [the recent war] will take place" (Alan Cranston, *The Killing of the Peace* ([Viking Press, 1945], 149). That was 1919, exactly 20 years prior to the beginning of World War II.

23. Cranston, *The Killing of the Peace,* 144–45.

24. Cranston, *The Killing of the Peace,* 145.

25. Cranston, *The Killing of the Peace,* 145.

26. Northedge, *The League of Nations,* 69.

27. Northedge, *The League of Nations,* 53.

28. Northedge, *The League of Nations,* 55, 83.

29. Northedge, *The League of Nations,* 83.

30. Northedge, *The League of Nations,* 54, 55.

31. Northedge, *The League of Nations,* 122.

32. Northedge, *The League of Nations,* 114.

33. Northedge, *The League of Nations,* 160.

34. Northedge, *The League of Nations,* 245.

35. Northedge, *The League of Nations,* 221, 267.

CHAPTER FOUR

1. F.S. Northedge, *The League of Nations: Its Life and Times 1920–1946* (New York: Holmes and Meier, 1986), 252.

2. This according to Hedley Bull, *The Anarchical Society: A Study of Order in World Politics* (London: Macmillan, 1977), 46.

3. G. Lowes Dickinson, *The International Anarchy, 1904–14* (London: Allen and Unwin, [1926] 1937), 2, ix.

4. Dickinson, *The International Anarchy*, ix.

5. Dickinson, *The International Anarchy*, 493.

6. Frederick L. Schuman, *International Politics: An Introduction to the Western State System* (New York: McGraw-Hill, 1933), 642, 661–63, 828–30. Schuman continued to affirm this idea in the subsequent editions, the 7th of which appeared in 1969, and in other books.

7. Georg Schwarzenberger, *Power Politics: An Introduction to the Study of International Relations and Post-War Planning* (London: J. Cape, 1941), 430, 399.

8. Schwarzenberger, *Power Politics,* 401–04.

9. Robert C. Hilderbrand, *Dumbarton Oaks: The Origins of the United Nations and the Search for Postwar Security* (Chapel Hill: University of North Carolina Press, 1990), 1.

10. Northedge, *The League of Nations,* 279, 278.

11. Northedge, *The League of Nations,* 51.

12. Hilderbrand, *Dumbarton Oaks,* ix.

13. Preamble, Charter of the United Nations. It is important to emphasize that the focus here is on the UN's primary purpose, to prevent war, with brief attention to its secondary purpose, to protect human rights. In these areas it has largely been a failure. Some of the agencies of the United Nations, however, have done very good work.

14. Northedge, *The League of Nations,* 1.

15. Hilderbrand, *Dumbarton Oaks,* ix.

16. Hilderbrand, *Dumbarton Oaks,* x, 3.

17. Hilderbrand, *Dumbarton Oaks,* 246.

18. Hilderbrand, *Dumbarton Oaks,* 170, 215.

19 Hilderbrand, *Dumbarton Oaks,* 246.

20. Hilderbrand, *Dumbarton Oaks,* x.

21. Hilderbrand, *Dumbarton Oaks,* x.

22. Hilderbrand, *Dumbarton Oaks,* 3.

23. Hilderbrand, *Dumbarton Oaks,* 105.

24. Hilderbrand, *Dumbarton Oaks,* 3.

25. Maynes' statement, made during an interview, is quoted in Linda M. Fasulo, *Representing America* (New York: Praeger, 1984), 285; quoted in Rosemary Righter, *Utopia Lost: The United Nations and World Order* (New York: Twentieth Century Fund, 1995).

26. Hilderbrand, *Dumbarton Oaks,* 65.

27. Hilderbrand, *Dumbarton Oaks,* 143.

28. Hilderbrand, *Dumbarton Oaks,* 161–63.

29. Hilderbrand, *Dumbarton Oaks,* 130–31.

30. Neither China nor France was really a Great Power at that time. But the United States insisted on including China among the permanent members of the Security Council. Then Britain, thinking (probably correctly) that the US motive was to give itself an automatic second vote (at that time, it was still assumed that the US-supported Nationalists would defeat the Communists), insisted on including France, believing that it (Britain) would be able to count on France to vote with it.

31. Hilderbrand, *Dumbarton Oaks,* 183–84.

32. Hilderbrand, *Dumbarton Oaks,* 119.

33. Hilderbrand, *Dumbarton Oaks,* 256

34. Hilderbrand, *Dumbarton Oaks,* x, 3.

35. Thomas M Campbell, in *Masquerade Peace: America's UN Policy, 1944–1945* (Tallahassee: Florida State University Press, 1973), 2.

36. Joseph E. Schwartzberg, *Transforming the United Nations System: Design for a Workable World* (United Nations University Press, 2013).

CHAPTER FIVE

All books and articles in this chapter are by Reinhold Niebuhr unless otherwise indicated. "NDM I" stands for *The Nature and Destiny of Man: A Christian Interpretation, Vol. I, Human Nature.* "NDM II" stands for *The Nature and Destiny of Man, Vol. II, Human Destiny* (Scribner's 1941, 1949). This two-volume edition has retained the original pagination for volume II as well as Volume I.

1. Richard Wightman Fox, *Reinhold Niebuhr: A Biography* (NY: Pantheon, 1985), 11, 17, 20.

2. Fox, *Reinhold Niebuhr*, 38.

3   Fox, *Reinhold Niebuhr*, 34-35.

4. Fox, *Reinhold Niebuhr*, 23.

5. Fox, *Reinhold Niebuhr*, 54.

6. Fox, *Reinhold Niebuhr*, 78–79.

7. Fox, *Reinhold Niebuhr*, 82–83.

8. Fox, *Reinhold Niebuhr*, 48.

9. Fox, *Reinhold Niebuhr*, 64.

10. Fox, *Reinhold Niebuhr*, 294.

11. Fox, *Reinhold Niebuhr*, 212.

12. Fox, *Reinhold Niebuhr*, 234.

13. *The Nature and Destiny of Man: A Christian Interpretation, Vol. I, Human Nature* (Scribner's, 1941), (henceforth NDM I), 124.

14. NDM I, 127–28.

15. *Moral Man and Immoral Society* (Scribner's, 1932), 25–26.

16. *Man's Nature and His Communities: Essays on the Dynamics and Enigmas of Man's Personal and Social Existence* (Scribner's, 1965), 39.

17. *Christian Realism and Political Problems: Essays on Political, Social, Ethical, and Theological Themes* (Scribner's, 1953), 197.

18. *Does Civilization Need Religion? A Study in the Social and Limitations of Religion in Modern Life* (NY: Macmillan, 1928), 9.

19. NDM I: 99.

20. Charles W. Kegley and Robert W. Bretall, eds., *Reinhold Niebuhr: His Religious, Social, and Political Thought* (Macmillan, 1961), 448.

21. *Reflections on the End of an Era* (Scribner's, 1934), 200.

22. *The Nature and Destiny of Man, Vol. II, Human Destiny* (Scribner's, 1943), (henceforth NDM II), 299.

23. NDM II: 61.

24. NDM II: 229.

25. *Does Civilization Need Religion?* 201-02.

26. *Does Civilization Need Religion?* 209.

27. "Can Schweitzer Save Us from Russell," *Christian Century* XLII, 3 September 1925: 1093–95, at 1094.

28. Fox, *Reinhold Niebuhr*, 30.

29. Fox, *Reinhold Niebuhr*, 29–30.

30. Fox, *Reinhold Niebuhr*, 123, 117.

31. Niebuhr, "The Truth in Myths," in *Faith and Politics: A Commentary on Religious, Social, and Political Thought in a Technological Age* ed. Ronald H. Stone (G. Braziller, 1968), 29. Originally published in *The Nature of Religious Experience: Essays in Honor of Douglas Clyde Macintosh,"* ed. Eugene Garrett Bewkes and Julius Seelye Bixler (New York: Harper & Brothers, 1937).

32. NDM I: 129.

33. NDM I: 143.

34. NDM II: 63, 67.

35. H. Richard Niebuhr, *The Meaning of Revelation* (Macmillan, 1941), 93.

36. June Bingham, *Courage to Change: An Introduction to the Life and Thought of Reinhold Niebuhr* (Scribner's, 1961), 268.

37. Niebuhr, "Religion and Modern Knowledge," in Arthur H. Compton et al., *Man's Destiny in Eternity* (Beacon Press, 1949), 125.

38. Kegley and Bretall, "Intellectual Biography of Reinhold Niebuhr," in Kegley and Bretall, eds., *Reinhold Niebuhr*, 3–23, at 13–14.

39. NDM I: 131.

40. NDM I: 141.

41. *Does Civilization Need Religion?* 200; *Reflections on the End of an Era*, 197.

42. Fox, *Reinhold Niebuhr*, 84.

43. *Reflections on the End of an Era*, 281.

44. *An Interpretation of Christian Ethics* (Scribner's, 1935), 20–21, 31–32; *The Self and the Dramas of History* (Scribner's, 1955), 97; Kegley and Bretall, eds., *Reinhold Niebuhr*, 438, 446.

45. Niebuhr, "The Truth in Myths," 15–32, at 23.

46. *The Self and the Dramas of History*, 4; "The Truth in Myths," 23; "Reply," in Kegley and Bretall, eds., *Reinhold Niebuhr*, 447.

47. "Coherence, Incoherence, and Christian Faith," in *Christian Realism and Political Problems*, 178.

48. Niebuhr, "Intellectual Autobiography," in Kegley and Bretall, eds., *Reinhold Niebuhr*, 3–23, at 19.

49. Niebuhr, "Reply," in Kegley and Bretall, eds., *Reinhold Niebuhr*, 448.

50. "The Truth in Myths," 17.

51. "The Truth in Myths," 17.

52. "The Truth in Myths," 6.

53. NDM I: 134.

54. "The Truth in Myths," 21.

55. Niebuhr, "Optimism, Pessimism, and Religious Faith," in Brown, ed., *The Essential Reinhold Niebuhr*, 3–17, at 6.

56. *Does Civilization Need Religion?* 212.

57. *An Interpretation of Christian Ethics* (Meridian, [1935] 1956), 22, 15.

58. Alfred North Whitehead, *Science and the Modern World* (Free Press, 1967), 191–92.

59. "Optimism, Pessimism, and Religious Faith," 3–17, at 16.

60. Alfred North Whitehead, *Process and Reality: An Essay in Cosmology*, Corrected Edition, ed. David Ray Griffin and Donald W. Sherburne (Free Press, 1968), 348.

61. *An Interpretation of Christian Ethics*, 32–33; see also "The Truth in Myths," 19.

62. Alfred North Whitehead, *Religion in the Making*, 50, cited by Niebuhr in *Does Civilization Need Religion?* 197–98.

63. Anthony West, in June Bingham, *Courage to Change*, 235–36; H. A. Odegard, *Sin and Science: Reinhold Niebuhr as Political Theologian* (Antioch Press, 1956).

64. Henry Nelson Wieman, "A Religious Naturalist Looks at Reinhold Niebuhr," in Kegley and Bretall, eds., *Reinhold Niebuhr*, 334–43, at 340.

65. David Ray Griffin, "Whitehead and Niebuhr on God, Man, and the World," *Journal of Religion* 52 (April 1973), 149–75.

66. NDM I: 165–66.

67. *Beyond Tragedy: Essays on the Christian Interpretation of History* (Scribner's), 9, 149, 217–18.

68. NDM I: 133, 134.

69. NDM I: 134–35.

70. NDM I: 135.

71. Niebuhr, *Discerning the Signs of the Times: Sermons for Today and Tomorrow* (Scribner's, 1946), 134, 145.

72. Niebuhr, "Theology and Political Thought in the Western World," in *Faith and Politics*, 55–66, at 65.

73. Niebuhr, "History (God) Has Overtaken Us," *Love and Justice: Selections from the Shorter Writings of Reinhold Niebuhr,* ed. D. B. Robertson (Westminster/John Knox Press, 1957), 292–96.

74. Niebuhr, "Anglo-Saxon Destiny and Responsibility," in *Love and Justice,* 183–89.

75. Fox, *Reinhold Niebuhr,* 182.

76. Fox, *Reinhold Niebuhr,* 184.

77. Quoted in Eric Patterson, *Christianity and Power Politics: Christian Realism and Contemporary Political Dilemmas* (Palgrave Macmillan, 2008), 69.

78. Fox, *Reinhold Niebuhr,* 183.

79. Niebuhr, "The Power and Weakness of God," in *The Essential Reinhold Niebuhr,* ed. Robert McAfee Brown, 21–32, at 28.

80. NDM II: 29–30, 71.

81. NDM II: 71n.

82. NDM II: 9–10.

83. NDM II: 299.

84. Franklin Gamwell, "Reinhold Niebuhr's Theistic Ethic," *Journal of Religion* 54/4 (October 1974), 387–408, at 406.

85. NDM I: 17.

86. NDM I: 241.

87. NDM I: 244.

88. NDM I: 262.

89. NDM I: 181.

90. NDM I: 243n5.

91. NDM I: 263.

92. *Does Civilization Need Religion?* 7–12, 155, 214.

93. *Does Civilization Need Religion?* 11–13.

94. Joel Rosenthal, *Righteous Realists: Political Realism, Responsible*

Power, and American Culture in the Nuclear Age (Louisiana State University Press, 1991), xvi.

95. Fox, *Reinhold Niebuhr*, 277.

96. NDM II: 127–28.

97. Fox, *Reinhold Niebuhr*, 195.

98. Fox, *Reinhold Niebuhr*, 211.

99. Niebuhr, "History (God) Has Overtaken Us," in *Love and Justice*, 292–93.

100. Fox, *Reinhold Niebuhr*, 213.

101. NDM II: 285.

102. NDM II: 314–15.

103. "American Power and World Responsibility," *Love and Justice*, 200–06, at 200.

104. Niebuhr, "American Power," 205.

105. "Anglo-Saxon Destiny and Responsibility," *Love and Justice*, 185.

106. "Plans for World Organization," *Love and Justice*, 206–13, at 209.

107. "Anglo-Saxon Destiny," *Love and Justice*, 188.

108. NDM II: 268.

109. NDM II: 266.

110. NDM II: 259.

111. "The San Francisco Conference," *Love and Justice*, 213–17, at 215.

112. "Pacifism and the Use of Force," *Love and Justice*, 247–53, at 248.

113. NDM II: 249.

114. "American Power and World Responsibility," *Love and Justice*, 202.

115. NDM II: 249.

116. Reinhold Niebuhr, *The Children of Light and the Children of Darkness: A Vindication of Democracy and a Critique of Its Traditional Defense* (Scribner's 1944), xi.

117. *The Children of Light,* 9.

118. *The Children of Light,* 10.

119. *The Children of Light,* 7.

120. *The Children of Light,* 8–9, emphasis added.

121. *The Children of Light,* 11; emphasis added.

122. *The Children of Light,* 33.

123. *The Children of Light,* 38–39.

124. *The Children of Light,* 39.

125. "American Power and World Responsibility," *Love and Justice,* 202.

126. "American Power," 200.

127. "American Power," 205–06.

128. "Plans for World Organization," *Love and Justice,* 212–13.

129. "Anglo-Saxon Destiny," *Love and Justice,* 189.

130. "Do the State and Nation Belong to God or the Devil?" *Faith and Politics,* ed. Ronald H. Stone, 83–101, at 85.

131. NDM II: 19.

132. NDM II: 22.

133. NDM I: 255, 258–59.

134. NDM II: 72.

135. NDM II: 72.

136. NDM II: 29.

137. "Plans for World Organization," *Love and Justice,* 207.

138. "Plans for World Organization," 208, 207.

139. "Plans for World Organization," 208.

140. "Plans for World Organization," 207.

141. "Plans for World Organization," 210.

142. "Plans for World Organization," 210.

143. "Plans for World Organization," 210.

144. "Plans for World Organization," 210.

145. "Plans for World Organization," 211.

146. "Plans for World Organization," 211.

147. "Plans for World Organization," 211.

148. "Plans for World Organization," 211.

149. Of course, given representation by population in the House of Representatives, less populous states generally have *less* power to determine policies than do the more populous states. But, thanks to the bicameral system, in which there is also a Senate in which each state is *equally* represented, this imbalance is significantly attenuated.

150. "Plans for World Organization," 211.

151. "Plans for World Organization," 212.

152. "Plans for World Organization," 212.

153. "Plans for World Organization," 205.

154. "The Christian Faith and the World Crisis," *Love and Justice,* 279–85, at 285.

155. "The Atomic Bomb," *Love and Justice,* 232–45, at 234–35.

156. "The San Francisco Conference," *Love and Justice,* 215.

157. "The Conflict between Nations and Nations and Between Nations and God," *Love and Justice,* 161–66, at 163.

158. "One World or None," in *Christianity and Crisis,* 16 February 1948: 9–10.

159. Dexter Masters, ed., *One World or None: A Report to the Public on the Full Meaning of the Atomic Bomb* (NY: New Press, 1946). Lippman's contribution was entitled "International Control of Atomic Energy."

160. "One World or None," 9.

161. "One World or None," 9.

162. "One World or None," 9–10.

163. According to Fox, Niebuhr had embraced the balance-of-power position in 1947 (*Reinhold Niebuhr: A Biography*, 233).

164. "The Illusion of World Government," in *Christian Realism and Political Problems* (NY: Scribners, 1953). Published originally in *Foreign Affairs,* 1949).

165. "The Illusion of World Government," 15–17, 20, 25.

166. "The Illusion of World Government," 17, 22–23.

167. "The Illusion of World Government," 27–28.

168. "The Illusion of World Government," 29; "Can We Organize the World," *Love and Justice,* 216.

169. "The Illusion of World Government," 18.

170. "The Illusion of World Government," 30, 31.

171. "The Anomaly of European Socialism," in *Christian Realism and Political Problems,* 49; *An Interpretation of Christian Ethics,* Preface; *The Structure of Nations and Empires: A Study of the Recurring Patterns and Problems of the Political Order in Relation to the Unique Problems of the Nuclear Age* (Scribner's, 1959), 298.

172. *The Structure of Nations and Empires* (NY: Scribner's, 1959), 279.

173. Fox, *Reinhold Niebuhr,* 229.

174. Fox, *Reinhold Niebuhr,* 236.

175. Fox, *Reinhold Niebuhr,* 252.

176. Fox, *Reinhold Niebuhr,* 252, 254.

177. Fox, *Reinhold Niebuhr,* 254.

178. Fox, *Reinhold Niebuhr,* 285.

179. Fox, *Reinhold Niebuhr,* 140.

180. *Reflections on the End of an Era,* ix.

181. *Reflections on the End of an Era,* 234–38.

182. *Reflections on the End of an Era,* 284.

183. *Reflections on the End of an Era,* 279.

184. *Reflections on the End of an Era,* 283.

185. *Reflections on the End of an Era,* 284–85.

186. *Reflections on the End of an Era,* 294.

187. Fox, *Reinhold Niebuhr,* 180.

188. "Why the Christian Church Is Not Pacifist," in Robert McAfee Brown, ed., *The Essential Reinhold Niebuhr* (Yale University Press, 1986), 102–19, at 103.

189. "Why the Christian Church," 111–12.

190. NDM II: 29-30.

191. NDM II: 29.

192. NDM II: 55.

193. NDM II: 59.

194. NDM II: 67.

195. NDM II: 45.

196. NDM II: 46.

197. *Man's Nature and His Communities: Essays on the Dynamics and Enigmas of Man's Personal and Social Existence* (Scribner's, 1965), 41.

198. NDM II: 166.

199. NDM II: 169.

200. NDM II: 155.

201. NDM II: 318.

202. NDM II: 206.

203. NDM II: 148, emphasis added.

204. "Why Christianity Is Not Pacifist," *Christianity and Power Politics* (Scribner's, 1940), 109.

205. NDM II: 81.

206. NDM II: 155.

207. NDM I: 286.

208. *Beyond Tragedy,* 295–96.

209. NDM I: 16.

210. NDM I: 287.

211. NDM II: 89.

212. NDM II: 68.

213. NDM II: 57.

214. NDM II: 127.

215. NDM II: 25.

216. NDM II: 30.

217. NDM II: 43.

218. NDM II: 84n16.

219. NDM I: 163.

220. Fox, *Reinhold Niebuhr,* 240.

221. Fox, *Reinhold Niebuhr,* 240.

222. Fox, *Reinhold Niebuhr,* 41.

223. Niebuhr, "From Progress to Perplexity," in Huston Smith, ed., *The Search for America* (Englewood Cliffs, NJ: Prentice Hall, 1959), 135–46, at 144.

224. John C. Bennett, "Reinhold Niebuhr's Social Ethic: The Later Years," *Christianity and Crisis,* April 1982: 91–95, at 94; reprinted in Kegley and Bretall, eds., *Reinhold Niebuhr: His Religious, Social, and Political Thought,* 46–77, at 70.

225. Niebuhr, *The Structure of Nations and Empires: A Study of the Recurring Patterns and Problems of the Political Order in Relation to the Unique Problems of the Nuclear Age* (Scribner's, 1959), 297).

226. Niebuhr, "The Moral Insecurity of Our Security," *Christianity*

and Crisis, 6 January 1958: 177–78.

227. Niebuhr, *Christianity and Crisis,* 13 November 1961.

228. Niebuhr, *The Structure of Nations and Empires,* 291.

229. Robert Williams, "Christian Realism and 'the Bomb': Reinhold Niebuhr on the Dilemmas of a Nuclear Age," *Journal of Church and State* 2 (1986): 302.

230. NDM II: 207.

CHAPTER SIX

1. In accord with the principle of subsidiarity, this legislation would be, as David Held put it in *Democracy and the Global Order: From the Modern State to Cosmopolitan Governance* (Stanford University Press, 1995), "framework legislation," meaning "legislation which specifies the principles and objectives of cosmopolitan democratic law to be upheld, leaving the detailed implementation of these to those at 'lower' levels of governance" (255). Held's book is the single best resource for seeing why a commitment to democracy now requires moving to *global* democracy.

2. G. Lowes Dickinson, *The International Anarchy, 1904-14* (London: Allen and Unwin, [1926] 1937), 2.

3. This statement occurs in Dickinson's introduction to *A Project of Perpetual Peace: Rousseau's Essay,* trans. by Edith M. Nuttall, with an Introduction by G. Lowes Dickinson (London: Richard Cobden-Sanderson, 1917).

4. William McNeill, *The Pursuit of Power: Technology, Armed Forces, and Society Since AD 1000* (Chicago: University of Chicago Press, 1980), 383–84.

5. Ronald Glossop, *Confronting War: An Examination of Humanity's Most Pressing Problem* (Jefferson, NC: McFarland, [1982] 1995), vii.

6. Glossop, *Confronting War,* 44.

7. Sydney Lens, "World Government Reconsidered," *The Nation*, 17 September 1983.

8. Otto Nathan and Heinz Norden, *Einstein on Peace* (New York: Simon & Schuster, 1950), 405.

9. Nathan and Norden, *Einstein on Peace*, 415.

10. Nathan and Norden, *Einstein on Peace*, 513.

11. Nathan and Norden, *Einstein on Peace*, 564.

12. As discussed in Chapter 5, Reinhold Niebuhr himself admitted the bankruptcy of his position. Although Niebuhr defended nuclear deterrence, which relies on the credibility of the threat to retaliate massively if attacked, John Bennett reported that in his later years Niebuhr remarked more than once that, if a nuclear attack came, he wanted to be among the first to be killed, because he would not want to be involved in deciding what to do (John Bennett, "Niebuhr's Ethic: The Later Years," *Christianity & Crisis*, April 1982: 91–95, at 94).

13. Although some of Falk's writings seem to question the wisdom of working for global democracy in the sense of a global *government*, his warnings are more about the route than the goal. His clearest acknowledgment of the need for a constitutional government at the global level is in "The Pathways of Global Constitutionalism," in Richard A. Falk, Robert C. Johansen, and Samuel S. Kim, eds., *The Constitutional Foundations of World Peace* (Albany: State University of New York Press, 1993), 13–38.

14. Because most Political Realists have rejected world government, it is often thought that Political Realism as such opposes it. But this school as such only insists that, in the situation of international anarchy, the relations between states will be settled primarily on the basis of power, not law and morality. It is fully possible for thinkers to accept this proposition while calling for the war-system to be transcended through the creation of a global government based on law. For examples of realists who have done this, see Frederick L. Schuman, *The Commonwealth of Man:*

An Inquiry into Power Politics and World Government (London: Robert Hale, 1954), and Georg Schwarzenberger, *Power Politics: An Introduction to the Study of International Relations and Post-War Planning* (London: J. Cape, 1941). Schwarzenberger said: "Power politics, international anarchy and war are inseparable [and war's] antidote is international government" (430, 399).

15. Helen Caldicott, *The New Nuclear Danger: George W. Bush's Military-Industrial Complex* (New York: The New York Press, 2002).

16. Caldicott, *The New Nuclear Danger*, 11. More recently, right after the attacks of 9/11, America's nuclear missiles were put on the highest state of alert and Russia and other nuclear countries probably responded in kind, so that thousands of nuclear weapons were on hair-trigger alert (Caldicott, ix).

17. Quoted by Fred Pearce in "Earth at the Mercy of National Interests," *New Scientist* 134/1826 (1992): 4.

18. One of America's founding fathers, James Wilson, arguing to the need for a federal constitution to replace the Articles of Confederation, argued that one of the problems with the latter was "the want of an effectual control in the whole over its parts. What danger is there that the whole will unnecessarily sacrifice a part? But reverse the case, and leave the whole at the mercy of each part, and will not the general interest be continually sacrificed to local interests?" ("Debate on Veto of State Laws (June 8)," in American History: From Revolution to Reconstruction and Beyond (online)). Unless Wilson's warning is now taken to heart at the global level, the focus on local interests will continue to undermine the general interest until there are no human interests at all.

19. Michael Renner, "Assessing the Military's War on the Environment," Lester Brown et al., *State of the World 1991* (New York & London: W. W. Norton, 1991), 132–52.

20. Thomas Friedman, "Saudi Plight: Like Being Back in USSR," *Santa Barbara News-Press*, May 27, 2003.

21. Kenneth Waltz, *Man, the State, and War: A Theoretical Analysis* (New York: Columbia University Press, 1959), 15, 228.

22. Quoted by David Gauthier, *The Logic of Leviathan: The Moral and Political Theory of Thomas Hobbes* (Oxford: Clarendon, 1969), 211.

23. Gauthier, *The Logic of Leviathan,* 211.

24. Waltz, *Man, the State, and War,* 228.

25. Waltz, *Man, the State, and War,* 210–12.

26. *Einstein on Peace,* 570. Einstein's point was supported by Glossup, who said that a global government would be less likely to become tyrannical than a national government because it would have no external enemies: "the restriction of the rights of citizens is often justified on grounds that it is necessary to protect the nation from its external enemies" (*Confronting War,* 351).

27. See Richard Falk, *The Great Terror War* (New York: Olive Branch, 2003), Chs. 6 and 7.

28. See Glossup, *Confronting War,* 351, who added: "The same kind of concern [about dictatorship] was voiced by those who opposed the Constitution of the United States of America as a replacement for the Articles of Confederation." In relation to the fact that this concern about the US Federal Government has become a genuine concern in our time, the previous point about the absence of external enemies is relevant, especially combined with the fact that the US Constitution did *not* guard against plutocracy.

29. Robert Dahl, who in a previous generation was arguably America's leading authority on democracy, reported that in contrast with all the anxiety about the possibility of a tyranny of the majority, "Neither at the Constitutional Convention nor in the 'Federalist Papers' is much anxiety displayed over the dangers arising from minority tyranny" (*A Preface to Democratic Theory* [Chicago: University of Chicago Press, 1956], 9). With regard to the possibility of a tyranny of plutocrats in particular, James Madison, said Dahl, "wished to erect a political system that would guarantee

the liberties of certain minorities whose advantages of status, power, and wealth would, he thought, probably not be tolerated indefinitely by a constitutionally untrammeled majority" (31).

30. David C. Korten, *When Corporations Rule the World* (San Francisco: Berrett-Koehler, and West Hartford, CT: Kumarian Press, 1995), 58.

31. Korten, *When Corporations*, 58.

32. Korten, *When Corporations,* 59.

33. Paul Hawken, *The Ecology of Commerce: A Declaration of Sustainability* (New York: Harper Business, 1993), 108.

34. Linda Melvern, *A People Betrayed: The Role of the West in Rwanda's Genocide* (New York: Zed Books, 2000), 4-5, 219, 222–23, 233.

35. Melvern, *A People Betrayed*, 229.

36. Henry Shue, "Let Whatever is Smoldering Erupt? Conditional Sovereignty, Reviewable Intervention and Rwanda 1994," in *Between Sovereignty and Global Governance: The United Nations, the State, and Civil Society*, ed. Albert J. Paolini, Anthony P. Jarvis, and Christian Reus-Smith (New York: St. Martin's Press, 1998), 60–84, at 60–61.

37. Alain Destexhe, "The Shortcomings of the 'New Humanitarianism'," in *Between Sovereignty and Global Governance*, Paolini, et al., eds., 85–92, at 85, 92.

38. Richard A. Falk, *Human Rights and State Sovereignty* (New York and London: Holmes and Meier, 1981), 37–42. Although Falk lists seven "logics," they finally reduce down to these three.

39. The UN is finally only an agent of the states—ultimately of the most powerful state. As Immanuel Wallerstein said about the new world order that emerged in 1945: "We had in reality moved into the era of US hegemony in the world-system, in which US economic strength was overwhelming and during which the United States was able to establish the set of rules for the world-system that best advanced its interests. . . . The United Nations

was essentially assigned no role of any significance in the postwar geopolitical structure, except to be a sort of figleaf to all these arrangements" ("The New World Disorder: If the States Collapse, Can the Nations be United?" in Paolini et al., eds., *Between Sovereignty and Global Governance*, 171–85, at 174–75).

40. Of these five countries—France, Great Britain, Russia, China, and the US—China has been the least imperialistic. But China itself *is* an empire, which Beijing is now struggling to hold together, and its policies with regard to some regions, such as Tibet, are widely considered imperialistic by those regions. In the modern world, nevertheless, China was throughout the twentieth century much more a victim than an agent of imperialist policies.

41. See Gernot Köhler, *Global Apartheid* (New York: Institute for World Order, 1978); Titus Alexander, *Unraveling Global Apartheid: An Overview of World Politics* (Cambridge: Polity Press, 1996); Richard A. Falk, *On Humane Governance: Toward a New Global Politics* (University Park: Pennsylvania State University Press, 1995), 49–55; Thomas C. Schelling, "The Global Dimension," *Rethinking America's Security*, ed. Graham Allison and Gregory F. Treverton (New York: Norton, 1992), 196–210, at 200. The one surprising person here is Thomas Schelling, who has been an enthusiastic supporter of US imperial enterprises, such as the war in Vietnam. In fact, Schelling himself was evidently surprised. He reported that he found himself musing about a constitutional framework that would make the world as a whole somewhat analogous to a traditional nation state, which led him to ask "what actual nation, existing now or in the past, might such an incipient world state resemble? If we were to contemplate gradually relinquishing some measure of sovereignty in order to form not a more perfect union, but a more effective world legal structure, what familiar political entity might be our basis for comparison? I find my own answer stunning and embarrassing: South Africa." In spite of being stunned and embarrassed, however, Schelling recovered sufficiently to point out that America's task in such a world is to safeguard what we have.

42. By the UN General Assembly in 1973.

43. Köhler, *Global Apartheid*, 2, 6.

44. Rajni Kothari argued that poverty in the non-Western world, far from being rectified by Western-financed development, is actually "a consequence of a certain model of development" because "the colonial outreach of world capitalism gave rise to structures where the new phenomenon of poverty was a necessary concomitant of the pursuit of wealth globally" (*Poverty: Human Consciousness and the Amnesia of Development* [London: Zed Books, 1993], 2).

45. John B. Cobb, Jr., *The Earthist Challenge to Economism: A Theological Critique of the World Bank* (London: Macmillan, 1999), 83. These figures, which differ from those of some other authorities, were derived by Cobb from the World Bank's *World Development Report 1991* (New York: Oxford University Press, 1991), 204–05.

46. Tom Athanasiou, *Divided Planet: The Ecology of Rich and Poor* (Boston: Little, Brown, 1996), 53.

47. The fact that America regards itself as a Christian nation makes this realization even more staggering. In saying "blessed are the poor," Jesus's point was *not* that we should therefore create as many poor people as possible.

48. James Nickel, *Making Sense of Human Rights: Philosophical Reflections on the Universal Declaration of Human Rights* (Berkeley: University of California Press, 1987), 51.

49. Henry Shue, *Basic Rights: Subsistence, Affluence, and U.S. Foreign Policy* (Princeton University Press, 1996), 2nd edition, 18.

50. David C. Korten, *Globalizing Civil Society: Reclaiming Our Right to Power* (New York: Seven Stories Press, 1998), 25.

51. John McMurtry, *The Cancer Stage of Capitalism* (London and Sterling, VA: Pluto Press, 1999), 163.

52. R. J. Vincent, *Human Rights and International Relations* (Cambridge: Cambridge University Press, 1986), 127.

53. The continuation of the colonial pattern in today's *neocolonial*

system was predicted by Ludwell Denny, an American writer who, anticipating that the British empire would be replaced by America's, boasted in a 1930 book entitled *America Conquers Britain*: "We shall not make Britain's mistake. Too wise to try to govern the world, we shall merely own it" (quoted in Alexander, *Unraveling*, 148). This prescient description of America's global *neocolonial* empire shows the futility of Niall Ferguson's call in *Empire: How Britain Made the Modern World* for America to become a real empire like Britain was. As Walter LaFeber observed, the American empire "is more militarized and less responsible in the long run—it is, indeed, an empire without responsibility. Niall Ferguson's recent essays ... are quite beside the point when he keeps pleading that the United States should take over from the British Empire. We've never had any intention of doing that .... We don't want that kind of responsibility—our attention span is not long enough, and we want to spend our money on ourselves, not in Africa or the Middle East" (personal communication, June 5, 2003).

54. George F. Kennan, "Review of Current Trends: US Foreign Policy," Thomas H. Entzold and John Lewis Gaddis, eds., *Documents on American Policy and Strategy, 1945-1950* (New York: Columbia University Press), 226–28, at 226–27.

55. John McMurtry, *Unequal Freedoms: The Global Market as an Ethical System* (West Hartford: Kumarian Press, 1998). McMurtry's point, of course, is that it is an *immoral* "ethical system."

56. John B. Cobb, Jr., *The Earthist Challenge to Economism: A Theological Critique of the World Bank*, 28.

57. Cobb, *The Earthist Challenge to Economism*, 13–27.

58. Rodney Dobell, "Environmental Degradation and the Religion of the Market," in *Population, Consumption, and the Environment: Religious and Secular Responses*, ed. Harold Coward (Albany: State University of New York Press, 1995), 229–50. Dobell's essay focuses primarily on the point, also emphasized by Cobb, that what makes this religion especially destructive is its commitment to

never-ending economic growth. Because economic growth entails increased pollution and destruction of habitat, the commitment to never-ending growth is in fundamental conflict with the fact that the planet itself is finite. Present economic principles contradict basic ecological principles, as Herman Daly's writings have emphasized. See Daly, "The Steady State Economy: Postmodern Alternative to Growthmania," in David Ray Griffin, ed., *Spirituality and Society: Postmodern Visions* (Albany: State University of New York Press, 1988), 107–22; *Beyond Growth: The Economics of Sustainable Development* (Boston: Beacon, 1996); and (with John B. Cobb, Jr.), *For the Common Good: Redirecting the Economy toward Community, the Environment, and a Sustainable Future,* 2nd ed. (Boston: Beacon Press, 1994).

59. John McMurtry, *Unequal Freedoms: The Global Market as an Ethical System* (West Hartford, CT: Kumarian Press, 1998), 16; and *The Cancer Stage,* 14, 22–23. The idea that capitalism constitutes a new universal religion, with a new theology, was suggested many decades ago by Karl Polanyi in his classic study, *The Great Transformation* (Boston: Beacon Press, 1957), 130, 133. McMurtry, in describing further consequences of this economic theology, wrote: "It prescribes commandments that cannot be disobeyed without harsh punishments and terrors to the disobedient. . . . Nothing that occurs from its fundamental principles of human ordering can be doubted, however many innocents may suffer death and destruction from their impositions. Those who presume to question or repudiate it are agents of the evil conspiracy known to all free humanity. Any who seek to defy or replace it are to be warred against until redeemed or eradicated" (*The Cancer Stage,* 22).

60. Amartya Sen, "Globalization: Value and Ethics," *Journal of Legal Hermeneutics,* 2001.

61. John Kenneth Galbraith, *The Culture of Contentment* (New York: Houghton Mifflin, 1992).

62. William Leach, *The Land of Desire: Merchants, Power, and the Rise of a New American Culture* (New York: Pantheon Books, 1993), 13.

63. Lebow's statement, originally made in an essay in the *Journal of Retailing*, was quoted in Vance Packard's 1960 bestseller, *The Hidden Persuaders*.

64. Korten, *When Corporations*, 152.

65. Quoted in Alan Thein Durning, *How Much is Enough? The Consumer Society and the Future of the Earth* (New York: Norton, 1992), Ch. 10.

66. Korten, *When Corporations*, 152.

67. Korten, *The Post-Corporate World: Life After Capitalism* (San Francisco: Berrett-Koehler Publishers, and West Hartford, CT: Kumarian Press, 1999), 33.

68. Edward S. Herman and Robert W. McChesney, *The Global Media: The New Missionaries of Corporate Capitalism* (London and Washington: Cassell, 1997). It is important, incidentally, not to assume that criticism of corporate capitalism implies a rejection of a market economy. Indeed, Fernand Braudel said that we should "make an unequivocal distinction between the market economy and capitalism" (*Civilization and Capitalism: 15th–18th Centuries, Vol. III: The Perspective of the World* [Berkeley: University of California Press, 1992], 632). David Korten, building on Braudel's distinction, defines capitalism as "an economic and social regime in which the ownership and benefits of capital are appropriated by the few" (*The Post-Corporate World*, 39). Korten rejected capitalism thus defined not only because it involves "the triumph of the few over the many," which means plutocracy, but also because it undermines genuine markets, which, as Karl Polanyi said, work "to ensure the freedom of the consumer, to indicate the shifting of demand, to influence producers' income, and to serve as an instrument of accountancy" (Polanyi, *The Great Transformation* [Boston: Beacon Press, 1957], 252). This same point was made by John McMurtry, who argued that global capitalism is "opposed to the free market it claims to embody" (*The Cancer Stage*, 37).

69. Durning, *How Much is Enough?* 36.

70. The ways in which the mass media now thwart democracy are described in Robert W. McChesney, *Rich Media, Poor Democracy: Communication Politics in Dubious Times* (New York: New Press, 2000), and Dean Alger, *Megamedia: How Giant Corporations Dominate Mass Media, Distort Competition, and Endanger Democracy* (Rowman & Littlefield Publishers, 1998).

71. Lord Acton, *Essays*, ed. Rufus F. Fears (Liberty Classics, 1985), Vol. II: 383; as quoted in Garry Wills, *Papal Sin: Structures of Deceit* (New York: Doubleday, 2000), 2.

72. I am alluding here to the democratic "all-affected principle," according to which all people affected by some policy should have been participants in creating it. This principle is multiply and extremely violated in today's world in which, for example, the tiny island nations will be the first to be inundated by the rising sea-level, although they have made virtually no contribution to global warming and have been the leading advocates of the kinds of reductions in greenhouse emissions recommended by the IPCC.

73. Acton had in mind specifically the absolutism of the papacy, as Garry Wills pointed out (*Papal Sins*, 1–2.)

74. It is presupposed here that we are speaking only of our planet. Encounter with beings from other parts of the universe would again raise the tension between God's universal interests and the much more limited interests of our planet's governments. Even with regard to our planet, furthermore, there is the tension between the interests of human beings and all the other forms of life. From the viewpoint of a very enlightened self-interest, we would realize that interest in the long-range good of human civilization requires interest in acting so as to allow other species to survive and even thrive. But because human self-interest cannot be assumed to be *very* enlightened and focused on *long-term* concerns, there would be serious tensions regarding many questions, such as whether, in light of the demand for more living space for human beings created by a still-rising human population, retaining habitat for other primates and elephants is essential.

My own recommendation would be that the protections based on an ecological ethic should be written into the global constitution and that, furthermore, the global legislature should include representatives selected by the world's environmental NGOs. With regard to the possibility of agreement on an ecological ethic, I have elsewhere suggested a resolution of what has arguably been the most seemingly irreconcilable divide—that between "deep ecology," with its ecological egalitarianism, on the one hand, and the concern with higher mammals expressed by the "humane society" and the "animal rights" movement, on the other hand ("Whitehead's Deeply Ecological Worldview," in Mary Evelyn Tucker and John Grim, eds., *Worldviews and Ecology: Religion, Philosophy, and the Environment* [Maryknoll: Orbis Books, 1994], 190–206).

75. NDM II: 266.

76. *Love and Justice: Selections from the Shorter Writings of Reinhold Niebuhr*, ed. D. B. Robertson (Philadelphia: Westminster, 1957), 248.

77. Support for this project can be found in Pope John XXIII, who said: "Today the universal common good poses problems of world-wide dimension which cannot be adequately tackled or solved except by the efforts of . . . public authorities which are in a position to operate in an effective manner on a world-wide basis. The moral order itself, therefore, demands that such a form of public authority be established" (*Pacem in Terris,* Part 4).

78. The centrality of impartiality based on sympathy to the moral point of view is expressed even by many philosophers who do not explicitly affirm the ideal observer theory of morality. For example, Jürgen Habermas, Germany's leading political philosopher, says: "The moral point of view compels the participants to *transcend* the social and historical context of their particular form of life and particular community and adopt the perspective of *all* those possibly affected" (*Justification and Application: Remarks on Discourse Ethics,* trans. Ciaran Cronin [Cambridge: Polity, 1993], 24; emphasis original). We can attain this impartial

standpoint, he says, "only by extending the individual participant perspective in a *universal* fashion. Each of us must be able to place himself in the situation of all those who would be affected by the performance of a problematic action or the adoption of a questionable norm" (49). Habermas's description of what is required by the moral point of view shows the unlikelihood that any individual, especially any individual political leader, would rise to it—a problem of which Habermas is all too aware.

79. Reinhold Niebuhr, *The Children of Light and the Children of Darkness: A Vindication of Democracy and a Critique of Its Traditional Defense* (New York: Scribner's 1944), 9–10.

80. NDM II: 259.

81. This slogan is gratefully adapted from a similar claim made by Paul and Anne Ehrlich about population control. Although I agree with their claim, I see global democracy as the inclusive goal, apart from which effective measures to stop and even reverse population control will be enacted in few countries.

82. For example, Hans Morgenthau, generally considered the founding father of Political Realism in this country, said that the precondition for a global government would be a global society with much more uniformity in beliefs and values than we have now and will probably not have for another two centuries (*Politics Among Nations: The Struggle for Power and Peace*, 5th ed. [New York: Knopf, 1972]). Kenneth Waltz made the same point in saying that "the amount of force needed to hold a society together varies with the heterogeneity of the elements composing it," with the implication being that there is far too much heterogeneity in the world today for a global government to be held together without far more coercive force than would be acceptable (*Man, the State and War: A Theoretical Analysis* [New York: Columbia University Press, 1959], 228). And B. V. A. Röling argued that "states and peoples differ too much in interests and in values for 'one world' to be feasible. . . . 'One world' is impossible without an unacceptable dictatorial setting" ("Are Grotius' Ideas Obsolete

in an Expanded World?" in *Hugo Grotius and International Relations,* ed. Hedley Bull, Benedict Kingsbury, and Adam Roberts [Oxford: Clarendon, 1992], 281–99, at 294). These authors were evidently unaware that, as I explain in the text, a constitution for a global democratic government needs common agreement only on a rather abstract set of basic principles, which are already implicit in all the traditions. The extreme heterogeneity of the world's cultural traditions is, therefore, not an insuperable obstacle.

83. See David Ray Griffin, ed., *Deep Pluralism: Whiteheadian Philosophy and Religious Diversity* (Westminster John Knox Press, 2005). This volume is based on a conference oriented around the "complementary pluralism" pioneered by John B. Cobb Jr., which is expressed in his books *Beyond Dialogue: Toward a Mutual Transformation of Christianity and Buddhism* (Philadelphia: Fortress, 1982) and *Transforming Christianity and the World: A Way beyond Absolutism and Relativism*, ed. Paul F. Knitter (Maryknoll: Orbis, 1999).

84. On the distinction between moral and "scientific" Marxism, see Alvin W. Gouldner, *The Two Marxisms: Contradictions and Anomalies in the Development of Theory* (New York: Oxford University Press, 1980). In China, this moral Marxism is often called "practical Marxism," in distinction from "scientific" Marxism with its "dialectical materialism." On this, see "Contemporary Development of Marxist Philosophy in China," *Socialism and Democracy*, Spring, 2001, by Ouyang Kang, one of the China's leading Marxist philosophers.

85. Hans Küng, *A Global Ethic for Global Politics and Economics* (New York: Oxford University Press, 1998), 98–99.

86. Michael Walzer, *Thick and Thin: Moral Argument at Home and Abroad* (Notre Dame: University of Notre Dame Press, 1994), xi.

87. Walzer, *Thick and Thin*, 4, 18.

88. Walzer, *Thick and Thin*, 6.

89. Three books that exemplify this growing sense of what all the

religions have in common overagainst the present world order are *Yes to a Global Ethic*, ed. Hans Küng (New York: Continuum, 1996); *For All Life: Toward a Universal Declaration of a Global Ethic: An Interreligious Dialogue*, ed. Leonard Swidler (Ashland, OR: White Cloud Press, 1998); *Subverting Greed: Religious Perspectives on the Global Economy*, ed. Paul F. Knitter and Chandra Muzaffar (Maryknoll, NY: Orbis, 2002). This last book is especially interesting in that Knitter is a Roman Catholic theologian and Muzaffar is a Muslim. Knitter, incidentally, has made the concern for global liberation integral to his own writings about religious pluralism; see his *One Earth, Many Religions: Multifaith Dialogue and Global Responsibility* (Maryknoll, NY: Orbis, 1995), and *Jesus and the Other Names: Christian Mission and Global Responsibility* (Maryknoll: Orbis, 1996).

90. Walzer, *Thick and Thin*, 67–68.

91. Whitehead, *Adventures of Ideas* (New York: Free Press, 1967), 172.

92. This account is accepted, in fact, by Walzer, who endorsed a "naturalist" account of our common, thin morality, in distinction from a "cultural" account, which he accepts with regard to the differences between the various thick traditions (*Thick and Thin*, 17). In the framework in which Walzer was working, a "naturalist" account of basic moral principles stands in opposition not to a religious account but to a cultural account that would regard the principles as purely human inventions. The naturalist account affirms that the principles are somehow *in the nature of things*, as the "natural law" tradition has always held. A naturalist account is, therefore, a religious account.

93. Whitehead suggested that although it is neither possible nor desirable for the religions to attain "identity of detailed belief," it might be possible, "amid diversities of belief," to "reach a general agreement as to those elements, in intimate human experience and in general history, which ... exemplify ... the divine immanence" (*Adventures of Ideas*, 161). With regard to what these elements exemplifying the divine immanence are, he said: "There are experiences of ideals—of ideals entertained, of ideals aimed

at, of ideals achieved, of ideals defaced. This is the experience of the deity of the universe. . . . The universe is thus understood as including a source of ideals. The effective aspect of this source is deity as immanent in the present experience" (*Modes of Thought* [New York: Free Press, 1968], 103).

94. The recent discussion of this position has revolved primarily around the position of John Rawls, especially as articulated in his *Political Liberalism*, 2nd edition (New York: Columbia University, 1996).

95. See Robert T. Handy, *A Christian America: Protestant Hopes and Historical Realities*, 2nd edition (New York: Oxford University Press, 1984). Not all of the movements surveyed by Handy, I should add, were Fundamentalist.

96. I have argued this in "Morality and Scientific Naturalism: Overcoming the Conflicts," in *Philosophy of Religion in the New Century: Essays in Honor of Eugene Thomas Long*, ed. Jeremiah Hackett and Jerald Wallulis (Kluwer Publications, 2004), 81–104, and in "Theism and the Crisis in Moral Theory: Rethinking Modern Autonomy," in *Nature, Truth, and Value: Exploring the Thought of Frederick Ferré*, ed. George Allan and Merle Allshouse (Lanham, MD: Lexington Books, 2005), 199–220. John Rawls, incidentally, did not deny this point. He simply believed that we who have inherited a democratic tradition can justify the needed principles simply by appeal to this tradition. But the idea that moral principles cannot be otherwise grounded is one of the reasons why religious citizens cannot accept this type of liberalism as the basis for our political life.

97. The "everything" here refers to the various concerns of the moral NGOs, such as human rights, workers' rights, ecological sustainability, overcoming global apartheid, and overcoming war, as well as the religious dream of a society and, indeed, a world based on divine principles.

98. Quoted in G. Clarke Chapman, *Facing the Nuclear Heresy: A Call to Reformation* (Elgin, IL: Brethren Press, 1986), 50. Chapman's

book is a call for Christians to declare nuclear weapons a *status confessionis*. My own view is that nuclear weapons are now part and parcel of the world order based around sovereign states, so that the only way to eliminate the world of nuclear weapons is to overcome this world order through the creation of global democracy.

INDEX

Acheson, Dean, 68
Acton, Lord, 10, 134–35, 137, 154n4, 183n71, 183n73
Albrecht-Carrie, René 157n40, 157n41
Alexander, Titus, 178n41, 179–80n53
Alger, Dean, 182n70
Alighieri, Dante, 9, 12
Allan, George, 188n96
Allison, Graham, 178n41
Allshouse, Merle, 188n96
anarchical, anarchy, 1–7, 29
Athanasiou, Thomas, 179n46
atomic bomb (weapons), 30, 31, 86, 114. *See also* nuclear weapons.

Augustine, 62, 95
authority religion, 50
Bacevich, Andrew, 133
Barth, Karl, 50, 148–49
Bellah, Robert, 131
Bennett, John C., 106, 72n223, 174n12
Bergson, Henri, 52
Beveridge, Albert, 25
Bewkes, Eugene Garrett: 163n30
Bingham, June, 163n35, 165n62
Bixler, Julius Seelye, 163n30
Black, Anthony, 152n7
Bodin, Jean, 3–4, 152n6, 152n7, 152n11

Bohr, Niels, 87
Bonhoeffer, Dietrich, 148–49
Braudel, Fernand, 182n68
Bretall, Robert W., 163n19,
    164n37, 164n43, 164n45,
    164nn47–48, 165n63,
    172n223
Brown, Lester, 175n19
Brown, Michael E., 153n14,
    153n16, 153n17
Brown, Robert McAfee,
    161n54, 166n78, 171n187
Bull, Hedley, 151n2, 152n10,
    154n8, 159n2, 185n82
Bultmann, Rudolf, 53
Bunck, Julie Marie, 152n4,
    152n8
Bush, President George, 117
Bush, President George W.,
    118, 175n15
Butler, Nicholas Murray, 18,
    157n34

Caldicott, Helen, 116,
    175nn15–16
Calvin, Jean, 62, 95
Campbell, Thomas, 40,
    161n35
Caplan, Richard, 152n9
Chapman, G. Clarke, 188n98
Chopra, Jarat, 5, 153n13
Christian Realism, 44, 45–46
civilization, anarchical, 1–7
Claude, Inis, Jr., 153n17
Clinton, Bill, 117, 123

Cobb, John B., Jr., 129,
    179n45, 180n56–58,
    186n83
Coffin, Henry Sloane, 71
Compton, Arthur H., 163n36
Concert of Europe, 19–20
consistency, 51–52
cosmopolitanism, 15
Coward, Harold, 180–81n58
Cranston, Alan, 158n7,
    159nn22–25
Cronin, Ciaran, 184–85n78
Cruce, Emeric, 10

Dahl, Robert, 176n29
Daly, Herman, 180–81n58
De Vattel, Emmerich, 152n11
Denny, Ludwell, 179–80n53
Destexhe, Alain, 177n37
Dickinson, G. Lowes, 29–30,
    34, 113–14, 151n2,
    154–55n14, 160n3, 169n4,
    160n5, 173nn2–3
disarmament, 12, 17, 19, 24,
    26, 27–28, 30–31, 36–37,
    91
divine power, 46–47, 8,
    49, 50, 97, 108. See
    also omnipotence.
Dobell, Rodney, 130,
    80–81n58
domestic analogy, 15, 16, 18
Dumbarton Oaks, 39, 160n9
Durning, Alan Thein, 132,
    182n65, 182n69

Einstein, Albert, 87, 115–16, 120, 144, 176n26
Eddy, Sherwood, 43
Elshtain, Jean Bethke, 152n5, 152n7
Enzold, Thomas H., 180n54
Ehrlich, Anne, 185n81
Ehrlich, Paul, 185n81
evil, problem of, 49, 58, 62, 63, 78, 88–89, 97, 99, 104, 108

Falk, Richard, 116, 124, 174n13, 176n76, 177n38, 178n41
Fasulo, Linda M., 161n25
Fears, Rufus, 154n4, 183n71
federal, federation, 13, 14, 15, 16, 31, 35, 111–12, 120, 142, 156n27, 175n18
Feffer, John, 152n9
Ferguson, Niall, 179–80n53
Ferré, Frederick, 188n96
Fox, Richard Wightman, 162nn1–11, 163nn27–29, 164n41, 166nn74–75, 166n77, 166n94, 166nn96–97, 166n99, 170n162, 170nm172–178, 171n186, 172nn219–221
Foxley, Barbara, 154n8
Fowler, Michael Ross, 152n4, 152n8
freedom, 3, 14–15, 16, 17–18, 25, 33, 34, 36, 40, 45–46, 47, 52, 53–56, 63, 66, 98, 102, 148
Friedman, Thomas, 118, 175n20
Freud, Sigmund, 1

Gaddis, John Lewis, 180n54
Galbraith, John Kenneth, 130, 181n61
Gamwell, Franklin, 65, 166n83
Gauthier, David, 119–121, 175–76n22, 176n23
Gifford Lectures, 44, 70
Christian Realism, 44, 45
global anarchy, 29, 39, 83, 102, 105, 106,116, 133, 136, 140
global democracy, iii, 40, 74, 77, 80, 84, 85, 90, 94, 112, 113, 117, 125, 126, 132–33, 134, 139, 140, 141, 146, 147, 149, 173, 174n13, 185n81
global (world) government, 67, 71, 74, 76, 79, 81, 85–86
Glossop, Ronald, 114–16, 173n5–6, 176n26, 176n28
God and the world, 56–58, 59, 60–61, 62, 63–64, 65
Gouldner, Alvin W., 186n84
Griffin, David Ray, 151n1, 165n59, 165n64, 180–81n58, 186n83
Grim, John, 183-84n74

Gromyko, Andrei, 35
Grotius, Hugo, 11, 154n7,
    154n8, 185n82

Habermas, Jürgen,
    184–85n78
Hackett, Jeremy, 188n96
Handy, Robert T., 188n95
Haroutanian, Joseph, 62
Hartshorne, Charles, 63–64
Harvard University, 44
Hawken, Paul, 122, 177n33
Hayes, Rutherford, 122
Hegel, G. F., 76
Held, David, 6, 153n18, 173n1
Hemleben, Sylvester John,
    154n5, 154n12, 154n13,
    156n28, 157n39
Herman, Edward S., 182n68
Hilderbrand, Robert, 31–35,
    39, 160n9, 160n12,
    160nn15–19, 161nn20–24,
    161n26–29, 161nn31–34
Hinsley, F. H., 151n3, 154n14
Hitler, Adolf, 28
Hobbes, Thomas, 4, 10–11, 17,
    31, 74–75, 119–21, 154n6,
    154–55n14
Hoffman, Stanley, 154n14
Holbraad, Carsten, 157n38
Howlett, Charles F., 157n34

international anarchy, 29–31,
    69, 70, 71, 72, 77–78,
    86–87, 89, 113, 115, 120

international government, 17,
    23–24, 31, 175n

James, William, 69, 93
Jarvis, Anthony P., 177n36–37,
    177n39
Jesus, 48, 52, 69, 96, 97, 98,
    99,101, 107, 124, 128, 133,
    148, 179n47
Johansen, Robert C., 174n13
St. John, 69

Kang, Ouyang, 186n84
Kant, Immanuel, 13–17,
    19–20, 24, 34, 52,
    155n16, 155n18, 155n19,
    156nn20–23, 156nn25–27
Keeton, George, 21, 157–58n3
Kegley, Charles W., 163n19,
    164n37, 164n43, 164n45,
    164nn47–48, 165n63,
    172n223
Kennan, George, 68, 93, 128,
    180n54
Kim, Samuel S., 174n13
Kingdom (reign) of God, 65,
    95, 96, 98, 99
Kingsbury, Benedict, 185n82
Knitter, Paul, 186n83,
    186–87n89
Köhler, Gernot, 178n41,
    178n43
Korten, David, 127–28, 131–
    32, 177n30–32, 179n50,
    182n64, 182nn66–68

Kothari, Rajni, 178–79n44
Küng, Hans, 142, 186n85,
    186n89

Ladd, William, 17
LaFeber, Walter, 179–80n53
Layne, Christopher, 5–6,
    153n14
Leach, William, 130–31,
    181n62
League of Nations, 21–28, 29,
    31–32, 35
League to Enforce Peace, 22
Lebow, Victor, 131, 181n62
Lens, Sydney, 115, 173n7
Life magazine, 44, 89
Lincoln, Abraham, 122
Lippman, Walter, 68, 87–88,
    169n158
Locke, John, 12
Lodge, Henry Cabot, 22, 25,
    158n7
Long, Eugene Thomas,
    188n96
Lorimer, James, 17–18, 27, 34,
    156n29, 156n31, 156n32
Luther, Martin, 62, 74–75, 95,
    129
Lyons, Gene M., 152–53n12

Macintosh, Douglas Clyde,
    42, 50
Madison, James, 176n29
Mann, Thomas, 115
Mastanduno, Michael,

152–53n12
Masters, Dexter, 169n158
Mastnak, Tomaz, 4, 152n9
Maynes, Charles Williams, 36,
    161n25
McCarthy, Joseph, 92
McChesney, Robert W.,
    182n68, 182n70
McMurtry, John, 128–30,
    179n51, 180n55, 181n59,
    182n68
McNeill, William, 114, 116,
    173n4
Mearsheimer, John, 6, 153n17
Melvern, Linda, 123, 177n,
    n34–35
Messianism, 78–79, 98–99
mind-body relation, 45–47,
    49, 52
Mitrany, David, 21, 157n43,
    157n2
Morgenthau, Henry, 68,
    93–94, 185n82
Murphy, Cornelius F., Jr.,
    12, 18–19, 153n2, 154n3,
    154n9, 154n10, 154n11,
    156n30, 157n33, 157n37
Mussolini, Benito, 28
Muzaffar, Chandra, 187n89
myth, mythological, 50, 53,
    54

Napoleon, 19
Nathan, Otto, 174nn8–11
Nickel, James, 179n48

Niebuhr, H. R. (Helmut Richard), 43, 51, 62, 163n34, 171n12

Niebuhr, Reinhold, iii, Chapter 5 passim, 134–39, 161–73, 184n76, 185n79

Niebuhr, Ursula, 71

Nicaea, 69

Norden, Heinz, 174nn8–11

Northedge, F.S., 21–22, 29, 31, 33, 157n42, 157n1, 158n9, 159n19, 159n21, 159nn26–35, 159n1, 160n10, 160n11, 160n14

nuclear weapons, 72, 105–06, 107, 113, 114, 115, 116, 117, 120, 139, 175n16, 188–89n98. *See also* atomic bomb (weapons).

Nuttall, Edith M., 154–55n14, 173n3

Odegard, H.A., 165n62

omnipotence, 46, 49, 58, 62, 63, 64, 69, 108. *See also* divine power.

Oppenheim, Lassa, 18–19, 22, 34, 157n35, 158n4

Oppenheimer, Robert, 87

organic, organism, 46, 47, 53–56, 89

pacifism: traditional, 95; legal or Einsteinian, 144

Packard, Vance, 181n62

Paolini, Albert J., 177nn36–37, 177n39

paradox, 52, 53, 56, 57, 58, 59, 60, 67, 98, 102

Pascal, Blaise, 66

Patterson, Eric, 166n76

St. Paul, 52, 69, 95, 97

Pearce, Fred, 175n17

Penn, William, 12, 17, 34

Polanyi, Karl, 181n59, 182n68

Political Realism, 5–7, 31, 68, 79, 105, 153n15, 174n14

Pope John XXIII, 184n77

providence, 62, 88

Randsdall, Senator Joseph, 158n22

Rawls, John, 188n94, 188n96

Reader's Digest, 44, 89

Realism, Political, 5–7, 31, 68, 79, 105, 153n15, 174n14

reason, rationality, 45, 52–55, 56–57, 59–60, 63, 65, 67, 73

Reiss, Hans, 155n16, 156nn20–23, 156nn125–27

Renner, Michael, 175n19

Reus-Smith, Christian, 177nn36–37, 177n39

revelation, 50–51

Richter, Rosemary, 161n25

Ritschl, Albert, 52

Roberts, Adam, 185n82

Robertson, D.B., 165n75, 184n76

Röling, B.V.A., 154n8, 185n82

Roosevelt, Franklin Delano, 36

Roosevelt, Grace, 154n13, 154–55n14, 155n15

Roosevelt, Theodore, 22, 158n8

Rosenberg, Julius and Ethel, 92

Rosenthal, Joel, 68, 166n93

Rousseau, Jean-Jacques, 11, 13, 14, 16–17, 19, 23, 34, 154n8, 154–55n14, 158n10

Rovere, Richard, 44

Russell, Bertrand, 55

Sabatier, Auguste, 50

Saint-Pierre, Abbé, 13, 16

Schelling, Thomas C., 178n41

Schmookler, Andrew, 116

Schuman, Frederick, 30–31, 34, 160n6, 174–75n14

Schwarzberg, Joseph E., 40

Schwarzenberger, Georg, 30–31, 34, 160nn7–8, 174–75n14

Security Council, UN, 37–38, 84, 90, 125, 161n30

Sen, Amartya, 130, 181n60

Senate, US, 25–26

Shaw, George Bernard, 23, 158n11

Sherburne, Donald W., 165n59

Shipman, Guy Emery, 92

Shue, Henry, 123-24, 127, 177n36, 179n49

sinfulness, 46, 47, 48, 53, 61, 65–66, 95, 98, 101, 102–03, 105, 107

Smith, Huston, 172n222

Social Gospel, 43, 69, 70, 95

sovereign, sovereignty, 2–5, 6, 9, 10, 12, 13, 14, 23, 26, 33, 36, 62, 80, 82, 84, 89, 90, 98, 108, 114, 117, 151n3, 152nn7,11, 178n41, 189n98

Spinoza, Benedictus, 62

Stalin, Joseph, 33, 134

state of nature, 10–12, 15, 16, 155n14

Stearns, Stephen J., 158n19

Stone, Ronald H., 163n30, 168n29

Suganami, Hidemi, 155n24, 157n43, 157n2

Sunday, Billy, 43

supernaturalism, 46, 47–48, 49–50

Swidler, Leonard, 186n89

Time magazine, 44, 89

Treverton, Gregory F., 178n41

Troeltsch, Ernst, 50

Truman, Harry, 92

Trump, Donald, 118

Tucker, Mary Evelyn, 183–84n74

Twain, Mark, 93
tyranny, 39, 72, 73, 74, 83, 85, 91, 92, 100, 119, 176n29

United Nations (UN), 12, 29–40, 73, 86, 123
Union Theological Seminary, 43, 44, 71, 82, 90, 94, 124, 160n13, 177n39

Vaughn, Charles Edwyn, 158n10
Versailles, Treaty of, 22, 24, 25, 42
Vincent, John, 128, 179n52

Wallace, Henry, 92
Wallerstein, Immanuel, 177n39
Wallulis, Jerald, 188n96
Waltz, Kenneth, 119–20, 175n21, 176nn24–25, 185n82
Walzer, Michael, 142–44, 186nn86–88, 187n90, 187n92
war, 6, 9, 10, 11, 12, 13, 14, 15, 16, 17, 19, 20, 21, 22, 23, 24, 25, 29–30, 31, 32, 33, 34, 35, 37, 39, 42, 44, 47, 62, 68, 69, 70, 71, 72, 91, 92, 93, 97, 99, 104, 106, 107, 112–13, 114, 115, 118–19, 120, 137, 149, 155n14, 159n22, 160n13, 175n14
Weiss, Thomas, 5, 153n13

West, Anthony, 165n62
Westphalia, Westphalian, 4–5
Whitehead, Alfred North, 45, 54–61, 63-64, 67, 96, 145–46, 165n57, 165n59, 165n61, 183–84n74, 187n91, 187n93
Wieman, Henry Nelson, 59, 165n63
Williams, Senator John Sharp, 25–26
Williams, Robert, 173n228
Wills, Garry, 183n71, 183n73
Wilson, James, 175n18
Wilson, Presdient Woodrow, 22, 25, 158nn5, 6, 159n18, 159n20
Wolff, Christian, 152n11
Woolf, Leonard, 23–24, 158nn11–16, 158n19
Woolf, Virginia, 23
world court, 38
world government, 10, 15, 18, 70, 71, 76, 79, 81, 86, 87, 88, 89, 90, 91, 94, 100, 112, 115, 120, 156n27, 170n164, 174n7, 174n14
World War I, 18, 20, 21, 24, 42, 70, 92
World War II, 28, 31, 32, 33, 70, 86, 92, 93, 124, 131, 148, 159n22

Yale Divinity School, 41–42, 43
Yeltsin, President Boris, 117

Printed in Great Britain
by Amazon